GW00493057

Round Hall Nu

Company Law

AUSTRALIA

LBC Information Services
Sydney

CANADA AND THE USA

Carswell
Toronto

NEW ZEALAND

Brooker's
Wellington

SINGAPORE AND MALAYSIA

Thomson Information (S.E. Asia)
Singapore

Round Hall Nutshells

Company Law

Catherine McConville

SERIES EDITOR

Bruce Carolan

DUBLIN
ROUND HALL SWEET & MAXWELL
2001

Published in 2001 by
Round Hall Ltd
43 Fitzwilliam Place
Dublin 2
Ireland

Typeset by
Round Hall Ltd, Dublin

Printed by
ColourBooks, Dublin

ISBN 1-85800-172-2

CONTENTS

Table of Cases

xiv   *Company Law*

Table of Legislation

IRELAND

SECONDARY LEGISLATION

UNITED KINGDOM

E.U.

1. INTRODUCTION

1.1   Definition of a company

When a company is registered at the Companies Registration Office and receives its certificate of incorporation, the company acquires a legal identity of its own which is separate and distinct from that of the individual shareholders or members who make up the company. The company is essentially an artificial entity created for the purpose of conducting business. In the case of *Salomon v. Salomon & Co.* ([1897] A.C. 30), Lord MacNaghten said that:

> "the company is at law a different person from the subscribers to the memorandum; and, though it may be that after incorporation the business is precisely the same as it was before, and the same persons receive the profits, the company is not in law the agent of the subscribers or a trustee of them."

In the main, the company will be registered with limited liability for its members, which basically means that if the company runs out of finance, the individual members of the company will not be held liable for the debts of the company.

The companies referred to in this text are all registered under the Companies Acts 1963–99, which provide a legal framework for the operation of the company and, whilst providing the company with certain rights at law, also subject the company to the rules and regulations set out thereunder. Irish companies are also subject to the intervention of European legislation, decisions of the judiciary in interpreting the legislation and also the rules of professional organisations which operate in their relevant area of business.

1.2   Other methods of carrying on business

Whilst there are over 200,000 registered companies in Ireland today, many people still operate their day-to-day businesses as *sole traders, i.e.* they act completely on their own account, under their own name. Accordingly, they are personally liable for all debts which their business incurs. For some very small businesses, the cost of incorporation, (which is set at IR£50 by the Companies (Fees) Order 1997) is a deterrent and the family tradition may simply always have been to operate as a sole trader.

Partnership is another method of carrying on business and is particularly prevalent in the professions. Section 1 of the Partnership Act 1890 provides that a "partnership is the relation which exists between two or more persons carrying on business in common with a view to a profit". The partnership does not enjoy limited liability and accordingly the individual partners are joint and severally liable for each other's actions and the debts which accrue to the partnership. Partnerships derived from persons with mutual trust and confidence combining for business purposes and sharing the responsibility. Section 13 of the Companies (Amendment) Act 1982 provided that partnerships in the fields of law and accountancy could exceed 20 members, but in any other field there cannot be more than 20 members. Under the Limited Partnerships Act 1907, it is possible to form a partnership whereby one or more of the partners enjoy limited liability. These partnerships are somewhat rare, but may benefit from certain tax advantages. In order to allow for the limited liability of certain partners, one or more of the general partners must retain unlimited liability and it is forbidden for a partner with limited liability to partake in the management of the business. Essentially, the partner who invests in the business and acquires limited liability will be a "dormant partner" and perhaps needed the option of limited liability as an incentive to invest in the partnership.

1.3   The benefits of the company

When setting up a business, the entrepreneur will be made aware of the several advantages of incorporating the business and registering as a company under the Companies Acts 1963–99. It must be noted that since the enactment of the European Communities (Single-Member Private Limited Companies) Regulations 1994 (S.I. No. 275 of 1994) it has been legally permissible to form a company under the Acts with only one member. Prior to this date, many *de facto* single-member companies existed, whereby one person essentially owned the majority of the company shareholding, with perhaps a spouse owning a token 1 per cent of the company shareholding. A single member company must, however, have two listed directors.

The advantages of registering a business in the form of a company can be summarised as follows:

1.3.1   Limited liability
The majority of registered companies avail of the benefits of limited

liability. Limited liability puts a limit or ceiling on the responsibility of the members to pay the debts of the company if the company becomes insolvent. Therefore, if a company runs out of money, the members will not be held responsible for the debts of the company. Thus, the members do not have to pay an amount equal to the full debts of the company, but rather their liability is limited. In any company the limit is one which the owners will have agreed to when establishing the company or acquiring shares in it, *e.g.* if Peter owns 100 £1 fully paid-up shares in Grafton Ltd. and the company is wound up as insolvent, its creditors cannot claim against him for any of the company's unpaid debts. But if only 70p was paid up on each of those £1 shares then Peter's liability to the company, and through it, to its creditors, is the 30p outstanding on each individual share which he holds. In effect, it allows individuals to enter into business with a limited risk of loss in the event of the business failing. Essentially, limited liability provides that where an enterprise fails, the individual member or shareholder's private assets are not called upon to satisfy any debts of the creditors.

1.3.2   *Taxation purposes*

The differing tax treatment which companies receive as opposed to individuals and partnerships is a major consequence of incorporation. At different times there has been great divergence between corporate tax rates and personal tax rates. In the mid-1970s, corporation tax rates varied between 40 per cent and 50 per cent while personal tax rates were as high as 80 per cent. Now corporate tax rates are 28 per cent (25 per cent for the first £100,000) while top personal rates are 32 per cent plus levies. In these situations it is often preferable to shelter income in a corporate capacity as opposed to a personal capacity. There are also several tax incentives for trading as a company. There is a 10 per cent rate of tax for manufacturing companies and pension contributions for company directors are more favourable than for self-employed persons. There are also inbuilt tax incentives for employees of companies, which may not be open to employees of sole traders, *e.g.* buying into share option schemes.

1.3.3   *Borrowing*

Banks and lending institutions are more willing to lend money to companies than they are to individuals. The lending institution can create debentures over assets of the company as security for the loan provided. When a fixed or specific charge is created, the fixed assets of a business (*i.e.* land, buildings) are given as security for loans. This form of security may *also* be available to the individual, but the *floating charge* on the other hand is a form of security which can only be utilised by a company. A *"floating"* charge can be created over company property which can be transferred and used by the company in the course of its business *e.g.* its working capital. This is a huge benefit for a company, as it has secured a loan from an institution by giving as security that which it can still control and deal with. This method of securing loans is not readily available to unincorporated businesses, as the Bill of Sale (Ireland) Acts 1879–83 would deem the property used as security to be personal property and would invalidate such transactions if detailed inventories setting out the exact nature of the security were not attached to the debenture. In the case of the company, the property is not deemed to be personal and, therefore, these requirements need not be met.

1.3.4   Perpetual succession

A company outlives those within it, and its existence remains unaffected by the deaths or other incapacities of any or all of its members. When a sole trader dies, the business will have to be transferred to legatees under a will, etc. When a partner dies, the partnership is either automatically dissolved or the interest has to be dealt with between the other partners unless the partnership deed provides otherwise. Whereas with a registered company, the only change that is made is that the shares change hands – the company as a whole is not affected. A company will continue to exist despite the fact that there is a change in its membership.

1.3.5   Transferability of interests

It is easy to transfer interests in a company – the articles of association usually provide that the members of a company may freely transfer their interest to another person, thereby divesting themselves of liability in relation to the shares. The transferee simply steps into the shoes of the transferor. However, there may be some restriction in the articles that allow the directors of the company to have absolute discretion over to whom a body of shares are transferred. Where the shares in a company are transferred to a new member, the property belonging to the company does not have to be transferred, as the property remains vested in the company.

1.4   Types of companies

A registered company may be a public or a private company and it may be registered with limited or unlimited liability. If the company has limited liability, it may be limited by shares or by guarantee. Under section 33 of the Companies Act 1963 it was stated that to qualify as a *private company,* a company must have share capital, the right to transfer shares must be restricted, the number of members may not exceed 50 and there must be a prohibition on any invitation to the public to subscribe for shares or debentures of the company. A public company is defined in section 2 of the Companies (Amendment) Act 1983 as being a "company which is not a private company". A *public company* must have a minimum of seven members and there is no upper limit of members. It will invariably be registered with limited liability and will invite the public to subscribe for shares through their prospectus and will then float on the stock market, *e.g.* eircom plc. The *public limited company (or PLC)* is required by section 19 of the Companies (Amendment) Act 1983 to have a nominal share capital of at least £30,000 and its issued share capital must be paid up in money or money's worth to at least 25 per cent of the nominal value of the issued share capital. A *private company* is therefore a much smaller entity (members ranging from one to 50) and is invariably formed to avail of separate legal personality and limited liability. It can range in size from the small family company to the large city firm. Sections 10–12 of the Companies (Amendment) Act 1986 divide private companies into small, medium and large-sized companies, and establish different requirements for each in relation to the amount of information which must be provided to the Registrar of Companies in their annual accounts. Much less detail is required of a small company than a large company in the preparation of the annual accounts.

A company can be *limited by shares* (the most common type of company), where the liability of the shareholders for the debts of a company is limited to any amount unpaid on their shares. A *company limited by guarantee* is a company in which the members guarantee to pay its debts up to a certain limit in the event of the company being wound up. Such companies are fairly rare and are usually non-profit-making organisations, *e.g.* sports clubs. The members will not be required to provide the company with any finance, either at the time of formation or during the lifetime of the company, as the company is not going to trade or seek to make profits. Given that one of the main benefits of incorporation is limited liability, the formation of a company with unlimited liability is somewhat unusual – an *unlimited company* is very similar to a partnership in that the company members are liable for all of the debts of the company. The formation of an *unlimited liability company* was popular as a means of limiting tax liabilities as the company may hold the property on behalf of someone and does not, nor was it ever intended that it would, carry on business. However, section 42 of the Companies (Amendment) (No. 2) Act 1999, now requires a company to furnish the Registrar with sufficient evidence that when registered, it will carry on a business within the State.

1.5   Conversion

It is possible for companies that have been registered under one form to pass a resolution to convert to another form. Under sections 9(3)(e) and 10(1) of the Companies (Amendment) Act 1983, it is permissible for a *private company* to be re-registered as a *public company*, providing that the company meets all of the requirements in relation to the authorised minimum share capital, the amount of paid-up share capital and the value of the net assets. A *public company* can also convert to a *private company* by altering its articles of association to restrict the transfer of shares, limit the number of members and prohibit the public from subscribing for shares.

This decision to alter the articles must be taken by the company in general meeting and a *special resolution* is required, *i.e.* 75 per cent of the company voting for the alteration.

Under section 52 of the Companies (Amendment) Act 1983, a limited company can re-register as an *unlimited company*, yet the assent of *all* the members of the company is required as this alteration will have a great impact on the liabilities of the members. Under section 20 of the Companies Act 1963, as amended by section 53 of the Companies (Amendment) Act 1983, an unlimited company can re-register as a limited company, but a special resolution is required before this change can occur.

2. FORMATION OF A COMPANY

2.1 Registration

In order to register a company in Ireland today, it is necessary to prepare and submit a number of documents to the Registrar of Companies, whose office is at Parnell House, 14 Parnell Square, Dublin 1. The Registrar will then review these documents and if he is satisfied that all of the formalities have been complied with, he will issue a certificate of incorporation. Section 18(1) of the Companies Act 1963 provides that from the date mentioned in the certificate as the date of incorporation, the subscribers to the memorandum become in law a body corporate and section 19 of the Companies Act 1963 states that the certificate of incorporation is conclusive evidence of all statutory requirements being complied with. The documents required for submission to the Registrar are as follows:

- The *Memorandum of Association* – which is effectively the constitution of the new company and is a fundamental document. It will contain clauses setting out the name of the company, the objects of the company, the statement that the company has limited or unlimited liability, the amount of share capital which the company is to be registered with and an association clause which binds the members of the company together.
- The *Articles of Association* – which set out the management rules of the company. Table A in the Schedule to the Companies Act 1963 sets out a schedule of Model Rules which will apply to the new company if no Articles of Association are registered. Usually, the promoters of the new company employ the Model Articles of Association in their entirety, or with modified amendments.
- A *Statutory Declaration* by either a solicitor involved in forming the company or, by a person designated as a first director or secretary, that all the requirements of the Companies Acts have been complied with (section 5, 1983 Act).
- A *Statement of Particulars* naming the first directors of the company and providing their addresses, nationali-

7

ties, occupations and details of any other directorships. The Statement should also provide similar details regarding the secretary of the company and should state the address of the registered office of the company (section 3, 1982 Act). This Statement must be signed by, or on behalf of, the subscribers to the memorandum and must be accompanied by a consent signed by each of the parties named in it as a director or secretary.

- A *Statement of the company's assets, liabilities and expenses* in order to assess the amount of capital duty which is to be paid on the formation of the company. The rates of capital duty are governed by sections 69–71 of the Finance Act 1973.

- A *Statutory Declaration* verifying that the company will carry on an activity within the State. This declaration is required by section 42 of the Companies (Amendment) (No. 2) Act 1999 and requires the promoters to set out the place or places in the State where the activity is to be carried on and the place where the central administration of the company will be carried on. This legislation is aimed at preventing companies with no Irish connections being registered within the State, as it has been suspected that many foreign companies may have been using their Irish registration to conceal their activities from the authorities in other states and thus evade tax or shelter money-laundering schemes.

- *Payment* of the necessary fee for registration, which is fixed at £50 by the Companies (Fees) Order 1997.

If all of the above is in order, the Registrar will issue the certificate of incorporation. He has final say in the process and it is noted that under section 21 of the Companies Act 1963 the Registrar can refuse to register a company where he is of the opinion that even the name of the company is undesirable.

Once the company is incorporated, it must publish certain details in *Iris Oifigiúil*, which is the official publication for company news. These details are required by Article 4 of the European Communities (Companies) Regulations 1973 which aims to have essential information concerning companies accessible throughout the E.U. The company must publish the fact that it submitted the memorandum and articles to the Registrar and that he in turn issued the certificate of incorporation. The address of the registered office and any changes therein must also be published. Article 10 of the Regulations provides that a failure to publish notice of these details will prevent the company from relying on the relevant documents and the fact of their existence as against a third party, unless the company can actually prove that the third party had knowledge of the documents.

2.2 The promoters

The promoters of a company are those individuals who have a role in forming the company and getting it up and running. A promoter was defined in *Twycross v. Grant* ((1877) 2 C.P.D. 469) as "one who undertakes to form a company with reference to a given project, and to set it going and who takes the necessary steps to accomplish that purpose". Whether or not a person is a promoter is a question of fact decided by the activities which he undertakes. The promoters of public companies can often be professional investment houses who specialise in establishing companies and attracting investment from the public. The promoter of a small private company will be the individual who takes the steps to incorporate his business into a limited liability company. Solicitors or accountants who are employed by the promoter to prepare the necessary documentation for registration will not be classified as promoters as they are merely acting in their professional capacity (*Re Great Wheel Poolgooth Ltd.* (1883) 53 LJ Ch. 42).

The promoter has great influence on the unborn company and its first transactions. There are great opportunities for the wayward promoter to make a profit for himself at the expense of the company. Promoters have therefore been subject to strict regulation and are deemed to owe *fiduciary duties* to the company they are forming, *i.e.* they are not permitted to make secret profits from transactions and must make full disclosure of all potential profits to the company as a whole. The promoter of a public company is therefore under very strict obligations to disclose in the prospectus all potential profits that are to be made to the public who are investing in the company. On the other hand, the promoters of a small private company may very often be the company's first directors and shareholders and therefore the disclosure of profits may effectively be made by the same persons to each other, whilst acting in different capacities. It has been established that the disclosure rule is satisfied once a promoter discloses an interest or a profit to "all the shareholders who ever were, or were likely to be, members of the company" (*Salomon v. Salomon* ([1897] A.C. 2)). It was also stated in the same case that "when all the shareholders are perfectly cognisant of the conditions under which the company is formed and the conditions of the purchase, it is impossible to contend that the company is being defrauded". In the case of *Erlanger v. New Sombrero Phosphate Company* ((1878) 3 A.C. 1218) it was stated that it was:

> "incumbent upon the promoters when forming a company to provide it with an executive i.e. with a board of directors who are aware that the property which they are asked to buy is the property of the promoters, and who shall be competent and impartial judges as to whether the purchase ought or ought not to be made."

This is basically saying that as long as there is an independent arm of the company, which is not a puppet of the promoter, available to scrutinise these disclosed transactions, then the disclosure rule has been satisfied and the promoter has fulfilled his duty, as the company as a whole is aware of the transaction and will accept it.

If a promoter was found to have sold property to the newly-founded company at a highly excessive price, thereby making a large undisclosed profit, without disclosure of ownership, then the contract for the sale of the property could be rescinded by the company. There is also some authority for saying that damages could be recovered on the basis of a claim for deceit or negligence on the part of the promoter. A promoter cannot set up a company and sell assets to the company at an overvalue, thereby making a profit for himself and in so doing deprive the company of profits.

Therefore, two rules are applied:

(1) If a company enters a transaction, in which a promoter has an interest, that transaction can be voidable at the behest of the company, unless they approve it after the promoter has made full disclosure of the interest which he may have.

(2) If the promoter did make a profit, it can be recovered by the company.

The idea is that any profit, however indirect or obscure, made by a promoter as a consequence of incorporating the company, must be disclosed; there are lots of others involved in the company now and one cannot be personally allowed to profit. In *Gluckstein v. Barnes* ([1900] A.C. 240) the promoters of the public company formed a syndicate and bought property in London for £140,000 and then sold the property to the new company which they were promoting for £180,000. They disclosed the £40,000 profit to the public who were subscribing for shares, but did not disclose a further £20,000 profit which had been acquired by them due to the fact that they had bought debentures in the company which had sold them the property at a below par rate and the liquidator of that company was paying off the debentures at par rate. It was held that there was inadequate disclosure to the company in this regard which left open the option of rescinding the contract or claiming damages.

The role of the promoter and the fiduciary obligations owed by him are more relevant in the promotion of public companies where the public at large stand to lose out if the promoter acts in a wayward manner. Professional promoters will require remuneration for the work which they have carried out in the promotion of the company. This may be in the form of an option to purchase the company's shares; commission; direct profit on sale of property to the company; or a fixed sum of money. The promoter of the private company, who will most likely be one of the number of first directors or shareholders, will probably see a paper profit in transferring the business to the company form. Article 80 of the Table A Articles of Association authorises the directors to pay the expenses incurred in promoting and registering the company. This is important because otherwise any agreement or contract made to pay a promoter before the company is actually incorporated is not binding on the company until such time as it is ratified by the company post-incorporation.

3. SEPARATE LEGAL PERSONALITY

3.1   The rule in *Salomon v. Salomon & Co. Ltd.*

It is a fundamental rule of company law that a company which is registered according to the Companies Acts has a distinct legal personality separate from its members. The most important consequence of this rule in the case of limited liability companies is that the shareholder is not liable for the debts of the company to its creditors (save to the extent of his liability to pay that which remains unpaid on the shares which were issued to him according to the terms of the articles and memorandum of association). The company is a separate entity at law and as such is capable of existence, independent of those members who make up the company.

The test case which established this principle was *Salomon v. Salomon & Co. Ltd.* ([1897] A.C. 22). In this case, Mr Salomon, having operated for years as a boot manufacturer, decided to transfer his business in its entirety to a newly registered company, owned and controlled by himself and his family. The business was therefore transferred to the company, who paid the sum of £39,000 for the acquisition. Part of the purchase price was to be satisfied through the issue by the company of 20,000 £1 shares to Mr Salomon and his nominees. The outstanding sum constituted a debt owed to Mr Salomon by the company, which was secured by the issue of a debenture to Mr Salomon over the assets of the company. When the company fell on hard times and went into liquidation, the debenture issued to Mr Salomon took priority over the claims of the company's unsecured creditors, *i.e.* he would get paid first out of the remaining proceeds of the company. The liquidator tried to claim that the company was merely the *agent* of Mr. Salomon, that Salomon was carrying on the business as before, through its agency and that accordingly he was personally liable for all the debts of the company. The House of Lords, however, held that the creditors had to respect the principles of incorporation and that the company could not be treated as an agent of the controller. The company was separate and distinct from those within it and legally had to be treated separately. It was immaterial that one individual controlled the company and that the other members were mere nominees, or, indeed, that the purpose of setting up the company was solely to avail of the limited liability protection. Companies, as such, are not in law the agents or trustees of their members, and their members are, not liable for their debts. Therefore:

(1) A modern registered company, if properly formed, is a legal person, separate and distinct from its members;

(2) Such a company is not *per se* the agent or trustee of its members; and

(3) The motives of those who formed it are not material to its subsequent rights and liabilities.

The fact of a company's separate legal personality leads to some awkward but nonetheless valid conclusions at law. An individual director of a company can employ himself even though he is also the controller of the company. Thus, in *Lee v. Lee's Air Farming Ltd.* ((1961) A.C. 12), cited with approval in *Re Dairy Lee Ltd.* ([1976] I.R. 314), the widow of a pilot was able to sue his company for worker's compensation after he had been killed in an air crash. Mr Lee as an employee was separate from Lee's Air Farming, the company which he had formed and run. In *A.G's Reference (No. 2 1984)* ([1984] 2 W.L.R 465), it was held that the controllers of a company who were acting dishonestly or illegally could be guilty of stealing from their company as the company is a distinct entity. In *Macaura v. Northern Assurance Co. Ltd.* ([1925] A.C. 619) damage to a company's property was not recoverable under an insurance policy because the policy was in the name of the company's controller and not that of the company. The controller did not have an insurable interest in the assets of the company and it was the company name which should have been on the policy, as it was the company who owned the property. In *Battle v. Irish Art Promotion Centre Ltd.* ([1968] I.R. 252), the plaintiff was the major shareholder and managing director of the defendant company and he sought to represent the company in court, as there were not sufficient funds to employ a legal team. As a consequence of a company's separate legal personality, only counsel or a solicitor could address the court on its behalf. The plaintiff, as a director of the company, was therefore unable to do so. In the English case of *Maclaine Watson & Company Ltd. v. Department of Trade and Industry* ([1989] 3 All E.R. 1056) it was stated that the *Salomon* case is as much law today as it was in 1897. In *Maclaine Watson*, a number of countries had set up the International Tin Council to regulate the price of tin, and it was to have all the legal capacities of a corporate body. When the council ran out of credit, the creditors sought to hold the member states liable for the debts, but the court held that the company was separate to all within it, and it was the company who had accrued the debts, so only the company was liable for those debts.

3.2   Modifications to the rule of separate legal personality

Whilst the cardinal principle of separate legal personality has been upheld by the courts over the years, there have been instances where the courts and the legislature set aside the principle of separate legal personality or restricted its operation to some extent. Legislation has been enacted over the years which seeks to apportion liability to those directors and members of a company who, through their actions, are seen to be abusing the principles of limited liability. By apportioning liability to persons within the company who have control within it, the legislation is disregarding to some extent the principle that the company is a separate and distinct entity from those who operate it. Provisions in the statutes which allow separate companies to be treated as *related companies* also disregard the separate legal personality of each individual company. The courts have also disregarded the *separateness* of the company in a variety of cases where they feel that the privilege of limited liability is being abused or where it is felt that two or more companies should be considered at law to be one entity, whether for reasons of control or where justice requires it.

3.3   Legislation

A number of provisions in the Companies Acts 1963–99 ignore the principle of separate legal personality of the company and do so in order to prevent the privilege of limited liability being abused. Section 297 of the Companies Act 1963 states that a director can be held criminally liable for fraudulent trading. Section 297(A) of the Companies Act 1963 as introduced by sections 137 and 138 of the Companies Act 1990 provides that a director of a company can be held personally liable for the debts of the company where he is found to have traded *fraudulently* or *recklessly*. Section 204 of the 1990 Act provides that personal liability can be attached to a director of a company that has been liquidated where there is evidence that the failure to keep books of accounts contributed to the winding-up. Section 39 of the Companies Act 1990 provides that where a company is wound up and is unable to pay its debts and the court sees that directors of the company may have taken loans from the company (something which is prohibited under section 31 of the 1990 Act), and that this contributed to the state of insolvency, then those directors can be brought before the courts and made personally liable for some or all of the debts of the company.

Other provisions in the Acts which deal with *related companies* also modify the principle of separate legal personality of the company to some extent. Whilst it is accepted that one company can be a subsidiary of another, *i.e.* that it is essentially controlled by the holding company, it is still recognised in law as a separate entity. However, certain legislation does impinge on the principle, *e.g.* section 150 of the Companies Act 1963 states that holding companies are required to lay the group accounts of *all* their companies before their annual general meetings. Section 140 of the Companies Act 1990 provides that other related companies within a group of companies can be required to contribute towards the liabilities of an insolvent company within the group. Section 9 of the Companies Act 1990 provides that a court-appointed inspector can investigate the affairs of related companies, *i.e.* companies whose affairs are linked to the company under investigation. All of these provisions manage to modify the cardinal principle that, once incorporated, a company is separate and distinct from any other company and from the persons within it.

3.4   The courts

The courts have seen fit to modify the principle of separate legal personality in a number of cases for certain reasons. First, the courts will not allow someone to use the privilege of incorporation and possibly set up a new company for a *fraudulent purpose*. If that is the case, the court will look behind the new company's separate existence and recognise that it has been merely set up as an instrument of fraud. Secondly, the courts will modify the principle if they feel that someone is attempting to abuse the privilege of incorporation by setting up a new company in order to *avoid a pre-existing legal obligation*. The courts have modified the principle to some extent whenever they look at two companies under the law of *agency* and feel that one is effectively controlled by the other as a matter of law and they have also modified the principle when they group a number of companies together and treat them as a *single economic entity*, because the justice of the case requires it.

3.4.1   Fraud/avoiding pre-existing obligations

In the case of *Cummins v. Stewart* ([1911] 1 I.R. 236), the defendant had
a licence agreement with the plaintiff which required him to pay roy-
alties to the plaintiff. In an attempt to avoid this agreement he transferred the licence to a company which had been formed for that purpose. The court said they could not ignore the fact that the company,
which by rights should enjoy separate legal personality from its members, had been set up as a sham. By incorporating a new company, the
promoter was abusing the privileges of incorporation and this could
not be tolerated by the courts. There was an attempt to destroy a legal
obligation and overthrow a legitimate claim. In *Creasey v. Breachwood
Motors Ltd.* ([1993] B.C.L.C. 480) a company called Breachwood Welwyn
Ltd., wrongfully dismissed Mr Creasey, its general manager. He then
commenced an action for wrongful dismissal against the company,
who then ceased trading, paid off all the creditors and transferred all
the assets to a new company called Breachwood Motors Ltd. Mr
Creasey had at this stage secured a judgment against Breachwood
Welwyn Ltd. which by then had no assets. Thus, the original company
had been able to escape a judgment against them by ceasing to exist,
but the court recognised that the new company had been set up by the
same people and that the transfer of assets and creation of the new
company had been to defraud Mr Creasey. The separate legal personality of the new company was disregarded and judgment was allowed
against it. In *Gilford Motor Co. Ltd. v. Horne* ([1933] Ch. 935), the defendant's contract of employment with the plaintiff had contained in
it a valid covenant prohibiting him from competing with the plaintiff
in that particular line of business after he left the plaintiff's employment. To avoid this covenant, the defendant set up another company
and commenced business in competition with the plaintiff. The defendant was neither a director nor overtly a shareholder of the company, nevertheless the company was controlled by him. The court
held here that the new company "was formed as a device, a sham to
mask the effective carrying on of the business by the defendant". An
injunction was granted restraining both the defendant and the new
company from carrying on business in competition with the plaintiff.
The court looked behind the company's separate legal personality. In
the case of *Jones v. Lipman* ([1962] 1 All E.R. 442), the defendant had
entered a contract to sell his house to the plaintiff. Then, in an attempt to avoid an action for specific performance by the plaintiff, he
transferred the house to a company formed by him. The court re-

fused to accept that the company was a separate legal entity and said that it had been created as "a device and a sham, a mask which he holds before his face in attempt to avoid recognition by the eye of equity".

As shown by the examples above, the court feels justified in disregarding the separate legal personality of the company where they feel that it has been set up purely for fraudulent, illegal or improper purposes. But there have been cases which show that whilst there may be a possibility that the company has been set up as a strategic move or to avoid higher tax levels, that does not allow the courts to set aside the separate legal personality, as there is nothing inherently wrong being done by the company. In *Roundabout Ltd. v. Beirne* ([1959] I.R. 423), the court felt that whilst a company had been set up by the owners of a public house to prevent the picketing of their premises by trade union members, there was nothing legally wrong with this "subterfuge". It did not warrant the court looking behind the new company. The owners of the public house wished to keep it as a "non-union" house and dismissed the staff who joined trade unions. When the unions threatened to picket the premises, the owners formed the new company and appointed new barmen as directors of the company. They then sought an injunction restraining the picketing, because the picket could not be lawful unless it was "in furtherance of a trade dispute". There was no trade dispute, as the new company had never employed any of the staff who had been dismissed and did not now have employees, but rather had directors managing the bar. The court accepted the argument and the case is thus an example where the court did not compromise or disregard the separate legal personality of the company because there was nothing inherently wrong with what they had done. It was essentially the using of a loophole to an advantage.

The same approach was used in the case of *Adams v. Cape Industries plc.* ((1990) B.C.L.C. 479) where it was argued that the defendant company, which presided over a number of companies involved in the mining of asbestos in South Africa, should be liable for judgments in the U.S. courts, because some of the companies in the group were set up solely to market the product in the U.S. The court felt that the separateness of the companies should not be compromised, even though it was quite clear that the framework of the companies and their inter-relationship was to separate the mining aspect of the business from the marketing aspect, and to thereby minimise the expo-

sure of the mining companies from problems on the marketing side.
There was nothing inherently wrong with doing this and, therefore,
the South African head company was not held liable for judgments
obtained against the U.S. companies in the States.

3.4.2   *Agency*

The courts have also disregarded the separate legal personality of each
individual company when they infer the relationship of agency or trust
between companies in the same group because of the special relationship which exists between what may be a holding company and one
of its subsidiaries. Once the courts find that a subsidiary is a mere
agent of the holding company, then their identities are combined and
they are treated as the one company. These holdings are at variance
with the *Salomon* principle and have to be accepted as being so. In
Smithstone & Knight v. Birmingham Corporation ([1939] 4 All E.R. 116),
the courts looked at the concept of agency. In this case the holding
company and the subsidiary wanted to be treated as the one company,
because it would entitle them to compensation. Under a Compulsory
Purchase Order, one could only get compensation if one owned the
land *and* carried on the business on the land. Here, the holding company owned the land, but the subsidiary carried on business on the
land. So were they two separate companies, and therefore legally independent, or were they essentially agents of one another? The courts
held that the subsidiary, even though it had a different name, etc. was
really an *agent* of the holding company, and therefore the courts held
that the two companies could be looked at as one entity. The courts
looked at the factors which exist where agency is imputed:

(a) whether the profits were treated as profits of the par-
     ent company;
(b) whether the persons conducting the business were ap-
     pointed by the parent company;
(c) whether the parent company was the head and brain
     of the business;
(d) whether the parent company governed the adventure;
(e) whether profits were made by the parent company's
     skill and direction; and
(f) whether the parent company was in *effectual and constant
     control.*

If the subsidiary is a mere theoretical existence then the courts will treat the subsidiary as an agent of the holding company as the agency is based on the idea of control. However, we must note that these principles could not be of general application, as a subsidiary could not always be held to be the agent of the parent company. It is felt that the inference of agency is often drawn by the courts in cases where any other holding would result in great tax avoidance. In *Firestone Tyne & Public Company v. Llewellin* ([1957] 1 All E.R. 561), agency was inferred as between an English subsidiary company and an American holding company, thereby requiring the American holding company to pay taxes in England on the profits of its *agent* subsidiary.

3.4.3   *Single economic entity*

In recent times the courts have put forward a further justification for disregarding the separate legal personalities of *related companies*. In such cases the courts disregard the separate legal personality of the company where justice requires it by regarding it as a mere constituent of a larger legal entity, or "single economic entity". This kind of disregard is different from the implied agency cases which disregard one body as being subsumed into another because of a control issue, whereas here justice requires that a number of companies all be regarded as one because practically this is the case. The justice of the case and what this entails may differ from case to case. In *DHN v. London Borough Tower Hamlets* ([1976] 3 All E.R. 462), Lord Denning said that where a corporate group exists, the court should look at the commercial reality of the arrangement where companies are actually bound hand and foot to each other. As a matter of commercial reality their separate character is disregarded and they are treated as one unit in law. In that case, three companies existed in a group with one *owning* the land interests of the group. The plaintiff company was a trading company and *occupied* the land for trading purposes. When the land was compulsorily acquired, the Land Tribunal said that there was no compensation payable as the company who owned the land had no business interest to lose. The compensation criteria required the company to own and have a business occupation of the property. However, the court saw the group of companies as one unit so that the plaintiff company was able to get full compensation.

In Ireland, Costello J. followed this line of reasoning in *Powers Supermarkets Ltd. v. Crumlin Investments Ltd.* (unreported, High Court,

June 22, 1981), where he treated a number of companies as one economic entity because the justice of the case required it and it was a
matter of practical, commercial reality. In this case, the first defendant
landlord had granted a lease of a unit in the shopping centre to the
plaintiff, and had entered a covenant with the plaintiff lessee not to
allow any person other than the plaintiff to trade as a grocery supermarket in the shopping centre. The first defendant then sold the shopping centre, by way of a transfer of shares, to another company called
Cornelscourt Shopping Centre Ltd., a company owned by the Dunnes
Stores Group, then conveyed a unit in the centre to Dunnes Stores
(Crumlin) Ltd. (the second defendant) which were not a party to the
covenant, and which commenced to trade as a grocery supermarket.
The plaintiff sought an injunction to restrain this trade. Both defendant companies were in fact wholly owned subsidiaries of the same
parent company, and it was established that in practice the controllers
of the group of companies, in their day-to-day activities, ignored the
formalities of the corporate structure. Costello J. held that the second
defendant should be treated as being bound by the covenant and he
granted the injunction sought, on the grounds that the justice of the
case required it, and that this decision accorded with the financial and
commercial realities of the case. Authorities have questioned the decision and asked whether it was necessary to set aside the corporate
personalities of each of the companies. Did the restrictive covenant
not restrict the covenantor's freedom to trade anyway and could the
same result not have been achieved by simply reading the covenant?
The *justice of the case* is a somewhat vague concept and it is hard to
assess when the courts will employ this thinking. It has been felt that
the separate personalities of the companies may be disregarded in
cases which would otherwise cause hardship to outsiders. Where the
companies themselves wish to be treated as the one entity for whatever advantage the courts may be slower to reach this conclusion.

In the case of *Allied Irish Coal Supplies Ltd. v. Powell Duffryn International Fuels Ltd.* ([1998] 2 I.R. 519), the Irish courts refused to lift the
corporate veil and see two companies as a single economic entity. Laffoy
J. in the High Court looked at the *Powers* case and said that the principle was not intended to be used in circumstances such as these. In the
case, the plaintiff company sought to join a parent company as a co-
defendant with its subsidiary (against whom the plaintiffs had brought
a claim for breach of contract). The plaintiff alleged that the companies were essentially one, and that the subsidiary was controlled by the

parent in all aspects of business. The defendants refuted this, stating that they were separate entities and that the subsidiary had its own substantial business. Laffoy J. held that the justice of the case did not require the separate legal entities of the companies to be disregarded. She felt that the claim of the plaintiff was really to render the assets of the parent company available to answer the subsidiary's liability. The Supreme Court agreed with this, saying that whilst a subsidiary could be dependent on the parent for finance, control and operations, it did not prevent it from being a separate legal entity. According to the court, the concept of limited liability was to enable some part of a person's affairs to be placed in a separate compartment and the principle of incorporation had to be respected.

3.4.4 Imputing characteristics

It is often said that the separate legal personality of a company is disregarded by looking at the controlling members of a company in order to characterise it, *i.e.* to attribute to it some characteristic, such as residence, negligence, or *mens rea*, which cannot be associated easily with a metaphysical being. However, the better view would state here that the separate legal personality is not being eroded, but simply that the character of those within it is being used to give it characteristics. Questions regarding the residence of a company arise frequently in relation to *taxation*. In these cases, the legal existence of the company is not ignored, but the separateness of its existence is compromised to the extent that the characteristics of its controllers are attributed to it, because its residence is assessed on the place of control. In *Unit Construction Ltd. v. Bullock* ([1960] A.C. 351), the court sought to ascertain the residence of the company on the basis of the residence of its controllers. Also, in *De Beers Consolidated Mines Ltd. v. Howe* ([1906] A.C. 455), Lord Loreburn spoke of a company not being able to eat or sleep, but it can keep house and do business, and the only way in which we can assess where it does this is by looking to the people behind it. Certain licensing statutes also require the applicant to be of good character. In a case of *The King (Cottingham) v. The Justices of County Cork* ([1906] 2 I.R. 415), a brewing company was looking for a wholesaler's licence and was therefore required to be of "good character". How could a company be of good character? The court held that the separate legal personality of the company would not be compromised if one were to assess the character of the company through those individuals who controlled the company. This is simply a matter of commercial practicality.

4. THE MEMORANDUM AND ARTICLES OF ASSOCIATION

4.1　Definitions

Every company registered under the Acts must have a memorandum and articles of association. These two documents are essential to the existence of the company and can be referred to as the constitution of the company. Whilst the memorandum contains the conditions on which the company is granted incorporation and the objects for which it is incorporated, the articles then set out the rules and regulations for the management and governance of the company. In the case of *Roper v. Ward* ([1981] I.L.R.M. 408), it was stated that the articles are subordinate to and are controlled by the memorandum as they cannot extend the ambit of the company's activities. These two documents must be furnished to the Registrar of Companies when the application for incorporation is made.

4.2　Memorandum of Association

Section 16 of the Companies Act 1963 provides that all registered companies must have a memorandum in the form as set out in the First Schedule to the Act. The category of the company will decide which form is to be followed, *e.g.* company limited by shares or company limited by guarantee. Section 6 of the Principal Act, then requires that the memorandum contain the following "obligatory clauses":

(1) the *name clause*
(2) the *objects clause*
(3) the *limited liability clause*
(4) the *capital clause*
(5) the *association clause*.

(1) The *name clause* must obviously state the company's name and, if the company is limited by shares or guarantee, the last word must be "limited". A name could be refused registration because it is too similar to another registered company's name. Section 23(2) of the 1963 Act provides that if, through inadvertence, a name has been registered which is identical or too similar to another registered company's name that the Minister can, within six months of registration, compel the

company to change its name. If such a direction is given, the company has six weeks to comply with the direction.

(2) The *objects clause* sets out the objects of the company, *i.e.* that which it is set up to do, and these will be decided by the promoters. If a company became involved in some form of transaction which was outside its objects, it is deemed to be acting *"ultra vires"*, *i.e.* outside of its capacity. Therefore, the *objects clause* in most private companies may well run into the hundreds in order to provide the company with as wide an ambit as possible. In the leading case of *Ashbury Railway Carriage & Iron Co. v. Riche* ((1875) LR 7 H.L. 653) Lord Cairns L.C. referred to the objects clause and said that it:

> "states affirmatively the ambit and extent of vitality and power which by law are given to the corporation, and it states, if it is necessary so to state, negatively, that nothing shall be done beyond that ambit, and that no attempt shall be made to use the corporate life for any other purpose than that which is so specified."

Therefore, a company which had as its object the making and selling of railway carriages did not have the authority *to build* a railway. The reasoning behind confining a company to those objects which were listed at the time of registration was to protect those shareholders who had invested at that time and who were felt to be entitled to see that their investment was used for the purposes for which they had intended. It was also to protect creditors who were deemed to have relied on the company's creditworthiness as based on the objects as set out. The *ultra vires* rule operated very strictly and caused great hardship to those third parties who entered contracts with the company which the company did not have the capacity to enter – as the third party was deemed to be aware of the lack of capacity of the company as the memorandum is a public document, *i.e.* available for inspection in the Companies Office. If the company did not have the capacity, the third party would not be able to enforce their contract as against the company. The rule was therefore mitigated in relation to such persons by section 8(1) of the Companies Act 1963 and Article 6 of the European Communities (Companies) Regulations 1973. This is discussed in Chapter 5.

4.2.1   Construction of the objects clause
Due to the strictness of the *ultra vires* rule, a number of rules of con-

struction were adopted by the draftsmen of the objects clause in order to extend the capacity of the company. Originally there was a
limiting rule known as the *"main objects rule"* which was set out in the
case of *Re German Date Coffee Co* ((1882) 20 Ch. D 169) and which said
that the first object listed was the main object and that all others were
then simply ancillary to and controlled by the first object. This was
therefore extremely limiting for the company and in the case of *Cotman
v. Brougham* ([1918] A.C. 514), it was held that if one included what
became known as an *"independent objects clause"* in the objects clause,
then that would have the effect of excluding the "main objects rule"
as each object would then be read separately and distinctly from any
other object listed. A second rule of thumb for the draftsman was to
include a clause which stated that the company could do "all such
things as are incidental or conducive to the attainment of the above
objects or any of them". This was also refined to allow the company
to do anything which "in the opinion of the directors could be carried
on advantageously in connection with its other objects or incidentally
thereto". This became known as a *"Bell Houses* Clause" as it was first
set out in the case of *Bell Houses Ltd v. City Wall Properties Ltd.* ([1966]
2 Q.B. 656) and could greatly extend what a company could do if the
directors thought it was in the best interests of the company. It has
been held in England that this is a subjective test, so that if the directors honestly believe that a certain proposal can be carried on with
benefit to the other objects, then such will be authorised, even if the
belief turns out to be misguided. These clauses will all be used as they
reduce the chance of a certain transaction being declared *ultra vires*.

It is important to distinguish between the objects and the powers
of a company. Any company which is incorporated and seeks to trade,
may state that it has an object of "borrowing money", but really this is
more of a power which is being expressly given to the company. Borrowing may not be an object of the company in the strict sense but it
is essential for any company to be able to do this. Therefore, the law
will readily imply such powers to a company which are necessary in
order to achieve the objects, *e.g.* employ staff, borrow capital, open a
bank account, institute and defend legal proceedings etc. Despite the
modification of the strict rules of construction and interpretation of
the objects clause, it is still common practice for a company to include
a vast array of objects in the objects clause, in order to avoid any
possibility of falling foul of the *ultra vires* rule.

4.2.2 *Alteration of the objects clause*

Up until the enactment of the Companies Act 1963 it was not possible to alter or amend the objects clause, except by court sanction. But section 10 of that Act specifically provides that a company can vote in general meeting to alter its objects clause and states that a special resolution is required for this vote to be passed, *i.e.* 75 per cent of the company must vote for the alteration. This does not mitigate the *ultra vires* rule in any way, because if the company went ahead and entered a transaction prior to voting for the alteration which would enable it to enter the transaction, then the act would still be *ultra vires*. But what section 10 does do is allow a company which wants to engage in new business to talk it over within the company and then vote for such a change. The company is not restricted to the objects it was registered with. There is a provision in section 10 providing that the dissenting minority who did not vote for alteration, can apply to the court within 21 days of the special resolution being passed to have the resolution set aside. The application must be made by the holders of at least 15 per cent of the issued share capital.

(3) The *liability* clause will, in the case of companies limited by shares or guarantee, simply state that the liability of the members is limited or in other instances it may state that the liability is unlimited.

(4) The *capital clause* must, in the case of a company limited by shares, set out the nominal share capital of the company, the number of shares into which the capital is divided and the amount of each share. The nominal capital of the company is the value in money of the shares which the company is authorised to issue. In the case of a private company, it will be a figure set by the promoters and will depend on the amount of funds the company will require. The amount of each share will be a nominal value, yet will vary in value depending on the success of the company. The company may increase the sum in its capital clause by passing a resolution to this effect. If it wishes to reduce its capital, this must be confirmed by the court as there is an interest in seeing that a company's capital remains intact.

(5) The *association clause* is simply a clause whereby those parties who subscribe to the memorandum agree to be formed as a company and all agree to take shares in the company. The subscribers' names will be listed and also the number of shares which they have taken and all subscribers shall sign their names.

Section 30 of the Companies Act 1963 requires the company to furnish any amendments which are made to its memorandum to the Registrar. As the memorandum is registered in the Companies Registration Office, this is necessary in order that the public may be aware of the amendments. The G1 Form is used for this purpose and failure to do this can result in a fine.

4.3   Articles of Association

The articles of association set out the rules and regulations for the management of the company. The articles will provide for the holding of meetings, the transfer of shares, the appointment of directors and their removal and the powers which are to be exercised by the directors. The articles therefore, *inter alia,* define the rights and obligations of the members of the company. Table A of the First Schedule to the Companies Act 1963 sets out a model form of articles of association, and most companies adopt these articles in their entirety or subject to some form of amendment. Where no separate articles of association are submitted (a company limited by shares or guarantee and *not* having a share capital need not register articles of association), then the model articles are applied to that company in their entirety. Where a company registers extra articles, these are added to the model articles, except in so far as the extra articles might vary the model articles.

The articles of association must be signed by each subscriber to the memorandum and are then stamped. Section 25(1) of the Companies Act 1963 provides that when the memorandum and articles are registered, they then bind the company and the members in a *contract* with each other, as if the memorandum and articles had been signed and sealed by each member and contained express covenants that each would be bound by the conditions and rules therein. The articles therefore create a contract between the company and the members but also between the members themselves, *i.e.* all have an interest in ensuring that the articles are obeyed. Therefore the company can seek to restrain breaches of the articles by the members and vice versa. A member could bring an action against the company for breach of the article which sets out his right to attend meetings and be given the requisite notice, or for breach of the article which provides that he has a right to be paid out a dividend once a dividend is declared. Essentially, the only rights which can be enforced by the member or against the member in terms of the "contract" are those which are granted to him in his *capacity as a member*. If a member of the company has a grievance in relation to their role as a director within the company, then they cannot seek to enforce that right by virtue of the section 25 contract. In the case of *Eley v. Positive Government Security Life Assurance Co* ((1876) 1 Ex. D. 20), the company's solicitor tried to enforce a clause in the articles against the company which restricted the company from terminating his employment as their solicitor. It was decided that although he was a member of the company, the right he was trying to enforce was not conferred on him as a member and he could not therefore rely on that clause as if it had set up a contract between himself and the company. Therefore, he had no redress. He would have needed a separate, formal contract restricting the company from terminating his employment. In *Isaac's Case* ([1892] 2 Ch. 158), this rule was modified slightly in that it allowed that if certain clauses were included in the articles, *e.g.* that the company solicitor is to be paid a certain fee, then if the solicitor acts in this matter, with no separate express contract, it will be implied that he is employed by the company, as this was the intention of the parties and he can therefore claim for what is due.

4.4   Alteration of the Articles

Section 15 of the Companies Acts 1963 provides that:

> "Subject to the provisions of this Act and to the conditions contained in its memorandum, a company may by special resolution alter or add to its articles. Any alteration or addition so made in the articles shall, subject to the provisions of this Act, be as valid as if originally contained therein, and be subject in like manner to alteration by special resolution."

The special resolution requires that 75 per cent of the company vote in favour of the alteration before it can be made and again emphasises the concept of majority rule. The company can alter its articles provided that the alteration is legal and in keeping with the memorandum. In the case of *Allen v. Gold Reefs of West Africa Ltd.* ([1900] 1 Ch. 65), a further proviso was added in that the company must exercise this power "in good faith for the benefit of the company as a whole". How do the courts assess when an alteration has been carried out in bad faith by the majority ? It would appear that the test is subjective and therefore in the case of *Shuttleworth v. Cox Bros. & Co.* ([1927] 2 KB 9), it was stated that a vote to alter was valid if the majority of the

members *honestly believed* that the alteration was in the interests of the
company as a whole. As a result of this thinking, alterations have been
upheld even where the minority may claim that the alteration has dis-
advantaged them. In *Greenhalgh v. Arderne Cinemas Ltd* ([1951] Ch. 286),
a minority shareholder argued that a decision of the majority to alter
an article which had originally provided that shareholders must first
offer the sale of their shares to existing shareholders before outsiders,
was invalid. He was obviously put out that shares could now be sold
immediately to outsiders as a result of the alteration. The court upheld the alteration as it was the majority will, and the fact that certain
shareholders were unhappy did not affect the validity of the vote. It
would appear that the alteration would have to have been undertaken
in bad faith causing some discrimination to the minority before the
court will set it aside. In *Clemens v. Clemens Bros. Ltd.* ([1976] 2 All E.R.
268), it was stated that, because each case differs, it is impossible to set
out hard and fast rules, but that perhaps majority shareholders' rights
are subject to equitable considerations which may make it unjust to
exercise them in a particular way. It can be noted that if the minority
interests are being disregarded or if there is oppression, they can take
an action under section 205 of the 1963 Act (See Chapter 7).

The case of *Allen v. Gold Reefs of West Africa Ltd* ([1900] 1 Ch. 65)
sets out that, because a company is given the right to alter its articles
by statute, it cannot therefore fetter its right to alter. Section 27 of the
Companies Act 1963 sets out that no member of the company can be
bound by an alteration of either the memorandum or the articles which
takes place after he becomes a member, but which increases his liability to contribute to the share capital, to pay further money to the
company or to take more shares than that which he now holds, as this
would be an unfair attack on his initial decision to invest and become
a member on certain terms.

4.5   Shareholders' agreements

It must be noted that it is a common business practice for shareholders within a company to enter into a shareholders' agreement between
themselves which can set out more specific regulations to be applied
in the particular company. This agreement would be supplemental to
the memorandum and articles of association and may be entered where
the members wish to include extra rights that would not be provided
to them if they relied solely on the articles and the Companies Acts
1963–99. The shareholders' agreement cannot be enforced against

the company unless the company has been included as a party to the agreement. A shareholders' agreement is often entered where minority shareholders wish to protect their position in excess of any protections contained in the articles of association or in statute.

5. THE CAPACITY OF THE COMPANY

5.1   The capacity to enter contracts

Given that a company has separate legal personality, it is capable of entering contracts *with other parties for valuable consideration.* Section 38 of the Companies Act 1963 provides that a company can enter three types of contract: written, oral and contracts under seal. In contracts where property is assigned, the company will have to apply its company seal to the contract, whereas in the standard contract, a party will sign the contract *on behalf of the company*, with the company's authority. The model articles of association provide that instruments to which the company seal is attached must be signed by a director and countersigned by another director or secretary, yet this could be altered by the individual company.

However, as noted in Chapter 4, the capacity of the company to contract is limited to that which is authorised by the *objects clause* in the memorandum of association. If a company enters a contract which is beyond its capacity, the contract will be deemed to be *ultra vires* and therefore void as between the company and its members, and also between the company and the third party who entered the contract with the company. This rule was extremely harsh for those third parties who did not know that the company was acting outside its capacity, and as a result were unable to have the contract performed. The *doctrine of constructive notice* also worked an injustice to these third parties, as the doctrine provided that those persons who deal with a company are *presumed to be aware* of the contents of the company's public documents, *i.e.* the memorandum and articles and are therefore affixed with notice of the fact that the company did not have capacity to enter the contract in question. These rules have been modified by statute in recent times and are discussed in this chapter.

5.2   Pre-incorporation contracts

Before discussing the issues that arise when the existing company enters contracts, it is important to note that a company cannot enter a contract until it has been incorporated and this date of incorporation is the date which appears on the certificate of incorporation. This is because the company is not deemed to exist prior to that date. Until section 37(1) of the Companies Act 1963 was passed, it was not possible to ratify a contract after incorporation, which had been entered prior to incorporation, but that section provides that:

"any contract or other transaction purporting to be entered into by a company prior to its formation or by any person on behalf of the company prior to its formation may be ratified by the company after its formation and thereupon the company shall become bound by it and entitled to the benefit thereof as if it had been in existence at the date of such contract or other transaction and had been a party thereto."

It is common for promoters and those involved in setting up the company to perhaps engage in contracts for supply, etc. at a stage when the company does not exist in law. This provision leaves it open to the company in general meeting to ratify the contract and give validity to the previous contract once incorporated. Until it is ratified, the contract is binding on the individual who purported to enter it on the company's behalf, but if the company itself does not want to ratify the contract then it can neither sue nor be sued on the contract. The third party will at least have a remedy against the individual. Under U.K. law (section 36(c) of the Companies Act 1985), the company cannot ratify the pre-incorporation contract, but rather the individual who entered it is held personally liable on the contract. In *HKN Invest OY v. Incotrade PVT Ltd.* ([1993] 3 I.R. 152), Costello J. held that where a controlling shareholder implemented the contract without any formal ratification, that was sufficient indication that the company wished to be bound by the contract, *i.e.* the contract was ratified by the conduct of the shareholder.

5.3 The *ultra vires* rule and the doctrine of constructive notice

The strict *ultra vires* rule, stating that a company had no capacity to enter a contract which was not expressly or impliedly provided for in the objects clause, was coupled with the principle that persons dealing with the company are presumed to be aware of the contents of its public documents, *i.e.* the articles and memorandum of association. This is the application of the legal principle of the *doctrine of constructive notice* which infers that because a person has access to the memorandum (including the objects clause) then they should be aware of the capacity of the company. They should make it their business to find out whether something is within the company's capacity or not, and cannot therefore seek to uphold the contract by pleading that they were unaware of the company's incapacity.

The case of *Re Jon Beauforte (London) Ltd* ([1953] Ch. 131) highlighted the harshness of the rule. The company's main object was to carry on business as a costumier, but nevertheless was involved in manufacturing veneer panels – an object which was not set out in its objects clause – and they entered into a contract with a third party for the supply of fuel to their factory to enable them to carry out the manufacture of the veneer panels. Because the company notepaper set out that the company was involved in the manufacture of veneer panels, the third party was taken to be aware that his fuel would be used for that purpose. Even though he had no idea that the company did not have capacity to carry on this business, he was assumed or deemed to be aware under the doctrine of constructive notice, *i.e.* the company's objects were public and he could have found out, so he was unable to recover the price of the fuel from the company as it was held that the contract was *ultra vires* the company and therefore void.

The legislature therefore intervened to mitigate the harshness of the doctrine and to protect innocent outsiders from the unjust effects of the *ultra vires* rule. Section 8(1) of the Companies Act 1963 will allow an outsider to rely on a contract which they entered into with the company, notwithstanding that the contract was outside the capacity of the company if:

(i)   the act/agreement in issue would have been lawful if the company had been authorised to do it in its objects clause;

(ii) the outsider was not *actually aware* at the time when he relied thereon, that the "act or thing" was *ultra vires* the power of the company.

Therefore, the outsider will be able to enforce the transaction as against the company, unless he knew at the time of making the contract that it was beyond the capacity of the company. The burden of proving the *actual awareness* would appear to rest with the company which is seeking to avoid the transaction. The outsider will show that he relied on the 'act or thing' in order to have the contract enforced.

The first point in section 8(1) simply provides that an outsider cannot rely on section 8 to uphold a contract that was not only *ultra vires*, but would not have been legal even if the act was sanctioned by the objects clause. In *Bank of Ireland Finance Ltd. v. Rockfield Ltd.* ([1979]

I.R. 21), the court looked at the claim of the plaintiff bank which sought to rely on section 8(1) to uphold a transaction which they had entered into with a company whereby they had loaned money to the company to purchase its own shares. The company was not authorised to borrow money for this purpose. The bank sought repayment of the loan, but they were not able to rely on section 8(1) because the transaction would not have been lawful even if the company was authorised to do it in the objects clause, under section 60 of the 1963 Act because a company cannot borrow money for the purchase of its own shares. Similarly, in *Re Frederick Inns* ([1991] I.L.R.M. 582; [1994] 1 I.L.R.M. 387), the courts found that a company could not make gratuitous payments when insolvent, so the Revenue could not rely on section 8(1) to uphold the payment.

The meaning of the phrase "actually aware" was examined in the case of *Northern Bank Finance Corporation Ltd. v. Quinn & Achates Investment Co.* ([1979] I.L.R.M. 221). In this case, the bank sought to rely on section 8(1) in order to uphold an agreement whereby the company had guaranteed a loan which the bank had given to a Mr Quinn. The bank obviously sought repayment of the loan, and the company sought to avoid the agreement by stating that the giving of a guarantee was outside the capacity of the company, *i.e.* not in its objects clause. The bank claimed that the agreement should be upheld under section 8(1) in that they were not *"actually aware"* of the company's lack of capacity. However, the court looked at the fact that the bank's solicitor had actually read through the memorandum and the articles. The bank stated that the solicitor had failed to understand the clause and thought that the company did have the capacity to guarantee the loan and that they were therefore not actually aware of the lack of capacity. But Keane J. effectively held that the bank had "actual notice" of the lack of capacity in that they had read the documents and were therefore actually aware and could not rely on the guarantee. The decision has been criticised in that Keane J. was confusing *"actual notice"* with *"actual awareness"*. The two are very different in legal terms, with notice connoting something less than full knowledge. A person is deemed to have notice of a matter when it is brought to his attention. When he then examines and reads it he will have actual knowledge, but in failing to understand what he reads, can it really be said that he has "actual awareness" of the matter?

European intervention also sought to mitigate the rule of *ultra vires* as it affects outsiders. Article 6 of the E.C. (Companies) Regulations 1973 (which implements the first E.E.C. Companies Directive) provides that an outsider could have an *ultra vires* contract upheld if:

(i)   they have entered the supposed contract with "an organ of the company, being its Board of Directors or any person registered under the regulations as a person authorised to bind the company"

(ii) they have entered the contract in "good faith".

The relationship of Article 6 with section 8(1) is unclear and it is felt that because Ireland already had enacted legislation in this regard, there was no need to implement Article 6 and that it was a legislative blunder to do so. Article 6 protection is limited to those contracts entered with the Board of Directors or a registered person, but it is felt by many that Article 6 may save an outsider who has read the memorandum but did not realise that it precluded capacity, provided that the outsider can show that he was acting in *good faith* and that Article 6 could therefore have a wider remit than section 8(1). The plaintiff outsider would be advised to plead both sections. In *International Sales and Agencies v. Marcus* ([1982] 3 All E.R. 551), the test of good faith was whether a party actually knew that he was involved in an *ultra vires* act or whether in all the circumstances it can be established that that party cannot have been unaware that this was an *ultra vires* act.

In the case of *Re Frederick Inns* ([1991] I.L.R.M. 582; [1994] 1 I.L.R.M. 387), the Revenue sought to uphold an *ultra vires* payment made to them by the company by attempting to rely on both section 8(1) and Article 6. They were unable to rely on section 8(1) because the payment which was made would not have been permitted by statute even if it had been within the company's capacity. The companies were all in one group and some had paid off the tax liabilities of the others. This was not permitted in company legislation. The Revenue were also prevented from relying on Article 6, because the agreement that had been struck was struck with the company's accountants and not its board of directors or a registered person, so it could not seek to have the contract upheld on those grounds.

5.4   Objects and powers

A contract may be wholly within the capacity of a company, *i.e.* it is clearly sanctioned by the company's objects clause and thus not affected by the *ultra vires* rule. However, if the directors of the company enter a contract for improper purposes which are not in the best interests of the company, or if the company borrows money as it is permitted to do in furtherance of its objects, but for an improper purpose not in its objects clause, those transactions can be declared void and unenforceable because the directors are abusing the powers endowed upon them, but the act is not *ultra vires* the company. The question of whether the company is pursuing an object of the company or merely using an ancillary power will have an effect on whether a transaction is deemed *ultra vires* or *intra vires*. The question of whether something is an object or a power will depend on the presence of an independent objects clause and a *Bell Houses* clause, *i.e.* is the act in question something which is an object, or is it a mere power which can only be used ancillary to the furtherance of an object and in the interests of the company? In the case of *Rolled Steel Products(Holdings) Ltd. v. British Steel Corporation & Co. Ltd.* ([1986] 1 Ch. 246), two directors of the company had caused the company to guarantee the debt of another company. The company was empowered in its objects clause to make such guarantees in such circumstances "as may seem expedient" and there was also an independent objects clause. It was held that the giving of the guarantees was "well capable of" falling within those objects. Slade L.J. examined the nature of objects and powers in relation to the *ultra vires* rule, saying that a company can only do that which is set out in the objects clause, or that which is reasonably incidental to the carrying out of these objects. He said, however, that where a particular act is of the category which is capable of being performed as being reasonably incidental to the pursuit of the objects, the fact that that power is used by the directors to attain some object not set out in the objects clause will not render that transaction *ultra vires*, but will merely be classified as an abuse of the powers by the directors and can be set aside by the company as an improper use of the company's powers.

Again, where an outsider enters this type of *intra vires* contract and has no reason to believe that the company is using its powers unlawfully, that contract will be upheld and is enforceable by the outsider. It is for the company to decide how to deal with the abuse of powers and it can ratify the contract if the company so decides, as it was not *ultra vires* to begin with. In *Rolled Steel Products(Holdings)* it was stressed that this abuse of powers .should not be confused with a transaction which is *ultra vires*. The former refers to whether those who concluded the transaction were using the company capacity for unlawful purposes whilst the latter concerns the very lack of capacity of the company to enter into transactions. This was upheld in Ireland by *Parkes & Sons Ltd v. Hong Kong and Shanghai Banking Corporation* ([1994] I.L.R.M. 341).

6. THE AUTHORITY OF THE CORPORATE AGENTS

In this chapter we will examine the situations whereby a contract may be wholly within the capacity of a company and not affected by the *ultra vires* rule, but the company may attempt to preclude the outsider from enforcing the contract as against the company because:

(a)   the person who entered into the contract on behalf of the company was *not authorised to do so*; or

(b)   some *formal requirement* has not been complied with and the contract cannot therefore be enforced, *e.g.* before the company can give a guarantee, it is set out in the articles that the members must pass a resolution, and this resolution is not passed.

However, both of these contracts may be enforceable by the outsider. In the first case, where the person who entered the contract on behalf of the company was not authorised, the contract may be enforced because the person so acting had *apparent or ostensible authority* to act on behalf of the company. In the second case, the outsider can enforce the contract because the formalities which were not complied with were matters which they could not possibly know of, as these matters are *internal management* matters. This is known as the rule in *Turquand's* case which mitigates the doctrine of constructive notice to a great extent, *i.e.* the outsider cannot be fixed with knowledge which he has no means of attaining.

6.1   Ostensible or apparent authority

The authority of the company is primarily vested in the members of the company but Article 80 of the model articles of association provides that the power can be delegated to the board of directors who are appointed. The board of directors will then act as agent for the company and can only act within the limits of the authority delegated to them. Article 112 of the model articles of association then provides that the board of directors can appoint a managing director and delegate authority to him. The company, as principal, is obviously bound if the agent had *actual authority* to conclude the contract on its behalf, *i.e.* the agent had specific written authority to enter into the specific transaction, but in a day-to-day business world it would not be possible to have agents acting under direct authority in all minor dealings. Therefore, the articles of association may set out that a managing director shall be appointed and by virtue of his role he will have the *actual authority* to carry out all every day transactions (*Hely-Hutchinson v. Brayhead Ltd.*([1968] 1 Q.B. 549)), *i.e.* he can act on behalf of the company in all matters. The common law has recognised that in everyday commercial affairs, it would grind matters to a halt if persons had to check the limits of an agent's actual authority before entering into an agreement with him, so the principle of *ostensible or usual authority* has been developed, *i.e.* a person dealing with an *agent* is entitled to rely on appearances without verifying the actuality. The principal is bound if the act is one within the ostensible authority of the agent. But of course, to rely on the doctrine, the outsider must *not have known or have had actual notice that the agent was exceeding his actual authority* as that would destroy the semblance of authority on which the outsider seeks to rely. In the sale of property, solicitors, estate agents and auctioneers would all have varying ranges of "usual authority" to act for clients and so, in the absence of notice of any restrictions on the usual authority, the principal will be bound by everything an agent does within his usual authority, even if the agent in fact is not authorised to act.

The conditions which have to be satisfied before one could rely on the principle of ostensible authority were set out in the case of *Freeman & Lockyer v. Buckhurst Park Properties Ltd* ([1964] 2 Q.B. 480):

(i) A representation that the agent had authority to enter the contract on behalf of the company must have been made to the outsider (*e.g.* that he previously had authority in that position).

(ii) The representation must have been made by a person or persons who had actual authority to manage the business of the company (*e.g.* in this case the board of directors effectively held the managing director up as the agent);

(iii) The outsider was induced by the representations to enter the contract and did rely upon it;

(iv) The company had the capacity to enter the contract to begin with.

In this case, the plaintiffs were a firm of architects who were suing the company for their fees. The company disputed payment saying that the contract had been entered into by a director who had not actually been appointed managing director, and it was therefore not within the director's authority to enter the contract. The articles had provided that a managing director be appointed, but this had not happened. However, the other directors had tacitly accepted that this particular director act in that capacity, without formal appointment. It was held that the director had ostensible or apparent authority to engage the plaintiffs since the board had tacitly represented that he was entitled to act as the managing director and such a contract was within the normal scope of the authority of such an agent. These principles have been accepted in Ireland in *Kett v. Shannon & English* ([1987] I.L.R.M. 36). The agent cannot appoint himself, so no representation by the agent can bind the company if the agent is not in a position within the company.

However, the doctrine of constructive notice could have an impact here, because the outsider is deemed to be aware of the company's public documentation and could be fixed with the duty of checking all of the formalities and checking whether a managing director was actually appointed, etc. This is why the courts have devised the following rule to relieve outsiders from the onus of having notice of the inner management matters of the company.

6.2   The rule in *Turquand's* case

The rule in *Royal British Bank v. Turquand* ((1856) 6 E. & B. 327) would say that whilst a person who contracts with the company is presumed to have read the public documents of the company and be aware of the capacity of the company, they are not expected to be aware of the internal workings of the company. These are the certain matters that an "outsider" will not be expected to know of, and therefore the existence of an irregularity in that matter will not prevent the "outsider" from upholding an otherwise valid contract. This rule relieves an outsider from any duty to satisfy themselves that any internal requirements necessary to *perfect* an agent's actual authority have been complied with, *e.g.* if a resolution is needed to sanction a particular contract, the outsider cannot be aware as to whether it was passed or not and therefore he can presume that it was.

In the named case, a company issued a bond under seal. The articles said that this could be done where an ordinary resolution was passed, so it was within the capacity of the company. However, no such resolution was passed. Later, the company said that the bond-holder could not enforce the bond as they had constructive notice of the requirement in the company articles that this ordinary resolution was required. The court rejected this and said that:

> "if an outsider read the articles they would see that an ordinary resolution was required - they could then infer that the resolution was so passed - they can't see into the internal workings of the company to see whether the resolution was so passed or not."

If it had been a special resolution that was required to validate the transaction then it would be different, because the outsider could inform himself if it was passed or not, as all special resolutions of the company must be registered, and are therefore public knowledge and the outsider would be deemed to have constructive notice of such (*Irvine v. Union Bank of Australia* ((1877) 2 A.C. 366)). The rule will only apply to those matters which are fully within the knowledge of the company. In *A.I.B. v. Ardmore Studios International Ltd. (1972)*, (unreported, High Court, May 30, 1973), the plaintiff bank was aware, by virtue of the articles, that the defendant company required two directors for a quorum, and that the company had only three directors. In attempting to renege on payment of a loan, the company said that the quorum had not been present at the meeting and therefore, the loan was invalid. The court said that this transaction fell within the "indoor management" rule and upheld the transaction.

Similarly, in *Ulster Investment Bank Ltd. v. Euro Estates Ltd.* ([1982] I.L.R.M. 57), the bank sought to receive repayment of a loan from the defendant company. The company brought up the issue of whether there had been a validation of the transaction in that the company's articles of association stated that two directors were required to form a quorum in ratifying any transaction, providing there be one "A" director and one "B" director. The company liquidator was seeking to avoid the repayment of the loan and stated that there had been an invalid quorum, as there had only been two "B" directors present, and that the bank ought to have been aware that it was an invalid meeting as they had a copy of the shareholders' agreement and the memorandum and articles. However, the court held that this was a matter within the internal management of the company and that the "outsider" was entitled to expect that the two directors who had signed the authorisation were fitting the requirements. Therefore, the Bank was able to rely on the transaction.

The outsider *cannot* rely on the rule in *Turquand's* case if documents setting out the irregularity become public, as they could then be aware of the irregularity. Also, if the party is actually aware that the internal workings were not complied with, *e.g.* a memo was sent to them making it clear that the requisite resolution was not passed, and the company are able to produce this, the rule in *Turquand's* case will be of no use to the outsider. In *Cox v. Dublin City Distillery* ([1915] I.R. 345), formalities had not been complied with in the issue of debentures to outsiders and to directors. The outsiders could rely on the rule in *Turquand's* case to uphold the transactions, but the directors could not, as they are deemed to be insiders.

The outsider would not be able to rely on the rule where certain matters relating to the transaction were unusual and should have put the outsider on the alert. In *Underwood v. Bank of Liverpool* ([1924] 1 K.B. 775), it was held that the fact that the director of the company was lodging cheques to his own personal account should have put the outsider on the alert that something was amiss about the transaction and he could not therefore rely on the rule.

The abolition of the doctrine of constructive notice in relation to *ultra vires* contracts by section 8(1) and Article 6 has made the existence of the rule less important, as the outsider can simply say that they have not read the documents to begin with and cannot therefore be aware of the rule, but it is still of use in the above scenarios.

7. THE COMPANY – TORTS AND CRIMES

7.1   Torts

A tort is a wrongful act which is perpetrated on someone and which invariably entitles them to seek damages. As a company is a legal entity, it is possible that a tort can be committed against it which would entitle the company to sue for damages, *e.g.* the tort of passing off would entitle a company to seek an injunction or damages due to the fact that another company is effectively usurping their business reputation. It is also the case that a company can sue for defamation where its business reputation has been damaged. Obviously the action is brought by the company itself, in the company name and that decision will have been arrived at in the general meeting or by the directors.

If someone acts negligently in relation to the company, then the company can claim damages, but it does not follow that the shareholders can also be entitled to recover damages as a result of the negligent act or omission. That could only be the case if the courts felt that there was some separate and distinct duty owed by the defendant to the shareholders. In *McSweeney v. Burke* (unreported, High Court, November 24, 1980), a consultant was sued by shareholders in a company in respect of financial advices given *to the company* which they had then relied on. Carroll J. said that in the instant case there was no negligence towards the company, but she also went on to say that the consultant owed no duty of care towards the shareholders, as his only client was the company itself. Essentially, the shareholders in the company should have got separate advice in relation to the transaction.

A company can also be deemed to commit a tort, and whilst the commission of the tort will not be in the objects clause, the company cannot seek to avoid liability in that regard for the negligent or tortious acts. In the case of an employer company, the company will be vicariously liable for the acts of their employees whilst the employees are acting in the course of their employment. The company may also be found to be directly liable for failing to have safety procedures, etc. in place. The company would also be deemed to have committed a tort where the directors or shareholders have authorised a tortious act. In this case, the court will look to the actions of the controllers to assess negligence. In *Lennard's Carrying Company v. Asiatic Petroleum Company* ([1915] A.C. 705), Viscount Haldane L.C. stated that:

"the fault or privity is the fault or privity of somebody who is not merely a servant or agent for whom the company is liable upon the footing of *respondeat superior*, but somebody for whom the company is liable because the action is the very action of the company itself."

In *The Lady Gwendolen* ([1965] 2 W.L.R. 91), the company was held liable in negligence for a collision as the ship was not using the radar facility. The ship's captain was not trained how to use radar and the Merchant Shipping Act 1894 would allow the liability of the company to be limited where the company was not at fault. In this case, the company was held to be at fault through the fact that the board had delegated responsibility to a manager who had not ensured correct safety procedures.

7.2 Crimes

A company cannot bring criminal prosecutions (unlike members of the public who can make the complaints). In *Cumann Luthchleas Teo. v. District Judge Windle* (unreported, Supreme Court, June 22, 1993), the Supreme Court found that Dublin Corporation could not attempt to bring proceedings to have the GAA prosecuted for breaches of the Fire Acts.

However, a company can be prosecuted for criminal acts, either personally or vicariously. Obviously, there are certain crimes which a company cannot commit. For example, bigamy and perjury can only be committed by the person actually charged with them. They cannot be committed by someone else acting on the accused's behalf. A company can only be punished by fine or sequestration of assets. A company can in certain circumstances be found personally liable for criminal acts and this is done by the courts identifying the acts and state of mind of the company's controllers and therefore establishing the *mens rea* for the crime. In many cases, however, it will be hard to assess whether a particular officer or employee within the company plays such an important role within the company that his acts and thoughts could be taken to be those of the company. In the one-person company, there would be no problem in imputing the intent of the controller onto the company. In *D.P.P. v. Kent & Sussex Contractors Ltd.* ([1944] K.B. 146), a company was held criminally liable for producing false petrol coupon returns because the act in question had been done by the only person through whom the company was capable of acting. A company can also be guilty of entering a conspiracy, as in the case of *Taylor v. Smith* ([1991] 1 I.R. 142), where the Supreme Court held that a company was guilty of entering into a conspiracy with the director even though the company was wholly controlled by him. Such a decision is reached by accepting that the parties are separate entities at law and a conspiracy could therefore be entered into which would deprive the company of assets. This contrasts with the English decision of *R v. McDonnell* ([1966] 1 Q.B. 233), which would say that two minds are necessary to engage in a conspiracy.

Where the "actor" within the company is lower down the ladder, it may be harder to impute their thoughts as being those of the company so as to make the company liable. In *Tesco Supermarkets Ltd. v. Natrass* ([1972] A.C. 153), the company had been charged with an offence under the Trade Descriptions Act. However, it was felt that the fault lay with one single manager, within one of the company's many stores, and it was not felt that he was the head and brains of the company so that his intention could be imputed to the company.

In England recently, there was an attempt to prosecute a ferry company for manslaughter arising from the "Herald of Free Enterprise" disaster in Zeebrugge but this was not successful. However, in *Jones v. DPP* (unreported, March 24, 2000), a Divisional Court in England ordered the DPP to reconsider a decision which held that a prosecution for manslaughter would not be brought against an allegedly negligent company employer. No doubt the liability would be pleaded on the basis that the company had unsafe procedures in place and the board did not satisfy themselves that safety measures were at a premium and did not employ managers to institute same. The evidence would have to be sufficient to bring the wrongdoing back to the corporate table.

8. SHARES AND MEMBERSHIP

8.1   Membership

The terms "*shareholder*" and "*member*" are synonymous in a private company limited by shares. When an individual acquires shares in a company, he becomes a shareholder and when his name is registered in the register of members, pursuant to section 31(2) of the 1963 Act, he becomes a member. Whilst all members of a company can have equal status, it is possible for the memorandum and articles to specify that some shareholders shall have "*preferential rights*" by virtue of the type of shares that they hold. If there are no such provisions in the memorandum and articles, then members will all have the same rights and will only be distinguished by the amount of shares that they hold, which will decide how many votes and how much control the shareholder can exercise in the company. The more shares one has, the more votes and control one will have.

There are four main ways in which an individual can become a member of a company:

(i)   by subscribing to the memorandum;
(ii)   by applying for an allotment of shares;
(iii) by receiving a transfer of shares from an existing member; and
(iv)   by receiving a transmission of shares on the death or bankruptcy of an existing member.

In the case of a subscriber to the memorandum, the law deems an individual to have agreed to become a member of the company by their conduct, and under section 31(1) of the 1963 Act, they become a member regardless of whether their names are entered in the register or not. As we have noted above, other shareholders *must* have their names entered on the register before they can become members in law.

8.2   Capacity

A minor, an individual under the age of 18 years, can become a member of a company by applying for an allotment of shares, by receiving a transfer from an existing shareholder or by receiving a transmission of shares on the death of a member. The minor then becomes liable to pay the amount left unpaid on the shares, but can also repudiate membership of the company whilst a minor or on attaining majority (becoming 18). The minor will then cease to be under any liability to the company. The reasoning here is that the minor may not have wished to become a member and must therefore act quickly to repudiate membership of the company and thus lose liability. A person of unsound mind can become a member of a company, but this membership can also be repudiated. A bankrupt can continue to be a member of a company, but the assignee becomes entitled to any payments or dividends to which the member would otherwise have been entitled.

8.3   Registration

Section 116(1) of the 1963 Act, as amended by section 20 of the Companies (Amendment) Act 1982 provides that the company must keep a register of its members, including all details of names, addresses, the number of shares held by the member, the amount paid on each share, the date on which the individual was registered as a member and the date on which they ceased to be a member. This register is to be open to the public for inspection at a fee and must be kept at the registered office of the company. The register is *prima facie* evidence of the matters referred to therein. This requirement seeks to provide transparency in relation to the ownership of shares and the amount of such ownership. However, the requirement for a public register cannot provide total transparency, due to the existence of section 123 of the 1963 Act, which states that the company may not enter notice of any trust on the register. This means that an individual could have a number of shares in a company, but they are held for him by a nominee and only the nominee's name appears on the register. Thus, an existing director or shareholder could have a secret shareholding in the company and be acquiring or purchasing these shares from others without other shareholders being aware of the level of their actual shareholding. Because this could be open to serious abuse, Part IV of the Companies Act 1990 imposes obligations on directors, secretaries and their families in relation to the disclosure of shareholdings. It also requires that individuals or groups must notify the public company when they have acquired any form of interest in shares amounting to over five per cent of the issued share capital. The company is also given the power to investigate the ownership of the company (section 81 of the 1990 Act) and the court is given the power to order that a particular individual disclose their full interests in a company's shares to any persons having a financial interest in the company. These provisions seek to prevent members of companies acquiring controlling interests in a company in an underhand manner and without the other members being aware of it.

8.4   Allotment of shares

When a company limited by shares is incorporated, it must allot shares to the persons who agreed to take a specified number of shares in the memorandum, *i.e.* the subscribers. It must then allot shares to those individuals who make an application for shares. The rules of contract apply to the application for shares and the subsequent allocation and acceptance by the applicant. Article 5 of the model articles of association would provide that the allotment of shares is entirely a matter for the directors of the company. However, section 20 of the 1983 Act states that the directors must be authorised to make the particular allotment of shares by a resolution of the company in general meeting or by the company's articles of association. The articles of the company will therefore generally provide the directors with a general authority to allot within a certain period, *e.g.* five years, and provide a maximum number of shares that can be allotted. This authority could be revoked by the company in general meeting even if this is not provided for in the articles, as statute would allow this. If a director allots shares in contravention of an authority to do so, the allotment will still be valid, but he will be subject to a fine of £2,500.

Section 23 of the 1983 Act provides that when a company is issuing new shares that the existing members can be given a "pre-emption right", *i.e.* that the company must give the existing shareholder a right of first refusal of the new issue of shares commensurate to the shareholder's existing shareholding. However, it is possible for an individual private company to omit this "pre-emption" right in its memorandum or articles. *Nash v. Lancegaye (Ireland) Ltd.* ((1958) 92 I.L.T.R. 11) provides that the directors must use their authority to allot new shares in "good faith".

Shares in a company may be issued to the shareholder for cash, in which case the shareholder becomes liable to pay the full nominal value of the shares allotted to him, either at the time of allotment or when a subsequent call is made for the shares to be fully paid up. Section 26 of the 1983 Act recognises that shares can be issued for consideration other than cash, *e.g.* for services or goodwill, and, if this is the case, the contract for the allotment of shares on this basis must be delivered to the Registrar of Companies for registration. If a public limited company issues shares for consideration other than cash, an independent report must be drawn up by a valuer, pursuant to section 30 of the 1983, Act valuing the consideration given.

In the case of public limited companies, 25 per cent of the nominal value of the share must be paid up at the time of allotment.

Whenever the company makes an allotment of shares, it must deliver all information on the allotments to the Registrar of Companies, including the names of the individuals to whom shares have been allotted, the amount of shares allotted and the amount paid up on each share. This information will also be placed on the company register of members, as these individuals will then become members.

Shares can be issued by the company at a *premium*. This means that the shareholder will pay an amount greater than the nominal value of the share. This makes sense when we think of the individual businessman who transfers his business to a company. The nominal value of the shares issued to him will be much lower than the amount he has actually given to the company, *i.e.* the transfer of the value of the business. The actual value of the share will be that which he has paid for it. However, this is deemed to be the issuing of shares at a premium, *i.e.* an amount in excess of their nominal value. The amount paid in, which represents the premium, must be paid into the share premium account and retained there because the capital of the company and cannot be considered to be company profits. Shares cannot be issued at a *discount* and this is set out in section 27 of the 1983 Act. The section also provides that where shares are allotted at a discount, that the allottee is liable to pay the remainder to the company, because otherwise the company is deprived of capital which should have been paid to it. Under section 87(1) of the 1963 Act, the shareholder must be issued with a share certificate setting out the amount of his shareholding. The share certificate is *prima facie* evidence of the member's entitlement to the shares.

8.5   Shares and shareholders

A shareholder to whom shares have been issued does not own any *specific portion* of the company by virtue of his ownership of the shares. The case of *Attorney General v. Jameson* ([1904] 2 I.R. 644) provides that the ownership of the shares gives the shareholder an interest in the *company as a whole* and this is essentially a property right in the company. The ownership of the shares confers certain rights upon the shareholder which are contractual as they are based upon the contract between the company and the member, set out in the articles of association pursuant to section 25 of the 1963 Act. By virtue of the articles, the shareholder has a number of individual rights within the company:

(i) the right to be paid a dividend, when the dividend is declared;

(ii) the right to attend the company meetings (and normally to vote at the meetings);

(iii) the right to participate in the distribution of the company assets, when the company has been wound up and the creditors paid off.

Any of these rights may be varied, or specifically added to, in a particular company's articles. The statute would also provide other rights to the shareholder, *e.g.* the right to petition the company in relation to certain matters and the right to inspect the company's books. These rights are personal to the individual shareholder and provide him with a right of action if they are breached in any way. (See Chapter 10).

The shareholder is required to pay up a certain amount on the allotment of the share to him, and may then be required to pay up the remaining amount when a "*call*" is made for payment. The model Articles 15–21 provide for the procedure for the making of calls. The liability of the shareholder is limited to the amount remaining unpaid on the nominal value of the share, *e.g.* a company may have an authorised share capital of £100,000 divided into 10,000 shares with a nominal value of £10 each. The shareholder is issued with 10 shares and his full payment to the company will be £100, but he may only have paid up £5 on each share to date. The remaining amount may be required on a call, or he will be required to pay up the final £5 on each share, upon the company being wound up.

If the shareholder does not pay up the remaining amount outstanding on the share, the company can forfeit the shares and the share capital of the company will therefore be reduced to the extent of the unpaid amount. Article 37 would then provide that the non-paying shareholder will cease to be a member of the company, but remains liable to pay the debt owed to the company. The shareholder could have also *surrendered* his shares, rather than have the company go to the trouble of forfeiting and the same rule applies in relation to his ceasing to be a member and remaining liable on the debt to the company.

It is also possible for a company to retain a *lien* over its shares by including a provision for this in the articles. The lien allows the company to have a hold over the share until the whole amount of the share is paid up. The lien is of no effective value, as the company has the more important right to forfeit the shares for failure to pay up on foot of a call, as set out above. However, liens have been enforced by companies in the past. In *G & S Doherty Ltd v. Doherty* (unreported, High Court, April 4, 1968) the court accepted that a lien could be enforced by the directors' attaching a term to a new issue of shares, stating that new shares would not be issued until existing shares were fully paid up.

8.6   Types of shares

It is possible for a company to create different classes of shares that have different rights attaching to them. These will be set out in the articles. All shares will *prima facie* be deemed to be of equal value and carry the same rights to a dividend, to vote and to participate in distribution of assets on winding up. The amount of the dividend paid will depend upon the amount of shares that the shareholder owns. However, the company can create different classes of shares and give preferential rights to the holders of a certain class of shares. These are known as preference shares. The rights attaching to these preference shares can be set out in the articles, which can obviously be altered by special resolution. However, it is the practice to include in the articles a provision which states that these preferential rights shall not be altered unless 75 per cent of that class of shareholders consent to the alteration. If there is no such provision, section 38 of the 1983 Act now provides that the 75 per cent vote of consent is required in order to alter the rights of the preference shareholders and that, if such a vote is passed, it is open to the holders of not less than 10 per cent of the preference shares to apply to court to have the alteration of their rights cancelled.

8.6.1   *The preference share*

The preference share usually provides its owner with the right to receive a fixed dividend amount, in priority to the holders of the other *ordinary shares, e.g.* the preference shareholder is guaranteed a five per cent dividend on the profits. The *preference share* may also provide that its owner shall have a right to participate in the capital available for distribution on winding up, in priority to other ordinary shareholders.

This type of share provides certain investors with a type of security in the company, *i.e.* guaranteed a fixed dividend and/or guaranteed first pick at the assets left over after winding up. Shares that do not have preferential rights attached are known as *ordinary shares*. The ordinary shareholder is entitled to a dividend when one is declared, and that dividend will be paid out of the profits after the preferential fixed dividend has been paid out.

8.6.2   *Preference as to a dividend*

Where a preference shareholder is given a right to a fixed percentage dividend on the profits, that dividend can only be paid where the profits for the particular year allow the correct payment to be made. If the profits were not adequate to make the payment at that time, the preference shareholder will seek to rely on the fact that the articles specify that the shares were cumulative and would allow the dividend to be paid off as soon as the profits permit, *e.g.* the following year. In *Webb v. Earle* ((1875) L.R. 20 Eq. 556), the court said the right would be deemed to be cumulative if the clause simply provided that the preference shareholder is to get the fixed percentage dividend. To make the right non-cumulative, the clause would have to specifically state this. The preferential dividend is to be paid out of profits whenever the dividend is declared by the directors. This is in contrast to the usual case where the dividend is declared by the company in general meeting. The directors will therefore only declare a preferential dividend when the profits are adequate and they will essentially be left with a discretion in this.

8.6.3   *Preference regarding capital*

It is also possible to issue preference shares which specifically provide that the shareholder will have preferential rights in relation to the participation in distribution of assets on winding up. In *Cork Electric Supply Co Ltd. v. Concannon* ([1932] I.R. 314), the court said that the preference shareholders in that case were allowed to have their capital returned in priority to the ordinary shareholders as this was specifically provided in the articles. However, there were then surplus assets left after all shareholders had been paid and it was held that there were no preferential rights applying any longer. All shareholders had equal rights as regards this surplus as there was no reference in the articles to this eventuality.

8.6.4   Voting and non-voting shares

A company could also divide shares into voting and non-voting shares. This would usually take the form of describing "A" shares and "B" shares, but the Stock Exchange does not approve of this division in shares whereby the right to vote is varied, as it is felt that in effect, those who own the company are not in a position to control it.

8.6.5   Redeemable shares

Section 207 of the 1990 Act permits companies to issue redeemable shares, provided that at least one-tenth of the issued share capital is non-redeemable. This permits the company to attract short-term investment capital and then pay it off when in a position to do so. To be redeemed, the share must be fully paid up and the company must then cancel the share or retain it as a treasury share. The share can be redeemed out of profits or from the proceeds of a fresh issue of shares. (See Chapter 14)

8.6.6   Transfer of shares

Shares can be transferred by the original shareholder to another party and this can be done freely unless the articles state otherwise. In all private companies, the right to transfer shares will be restricted by the articles, which may state that the directors can refuse to register the transfer of shares to a person of whom they do not approve or that shareholders who are transferring their shares must give the right of first refusal of those shares to existing shareholders. Both of these provisions restrain the free transfer of shares and protect against the extension of the small private company to other wider groups.

The first restriction is set out in Article 24 of the model articles and would be included in all Irish private companies. However, the directors must exercise this right to veto a transfer and refuse to register in good faith and for the benefit of the company as a whole. The court will allow the directors that discretion, yet if reasons for making the refusal are given, the court may consider whether they are reasonable or not. In *Re Hafner* ([1943] I.R. 426), it was stated that the court would only set aside the directors' refusal to register the transfer if it can be proven that this decision was made in bad faith. In that case, the directors had failed to register a transfer of 500 shares to the plaintiff. The shares had been transferred to the plaintiff by his uncle's personal representative and the plaintiff was claiming that there was an ulterior motive in refusing to recognise the transfer, *i.e.* that the directors were remunerating themselves from the profits at present and if the shares were transferred to the plaintiff, he would be in a position to challenge this.

The second restriction would simply set out in the articles that the shareholders shall not transfer shares to outsiders unless they have first asked whether any other shareholder wishes to purchase the shares.

Section 81 of the 1963 Act provides that, notwithstanding anything in the articles, it shall not be lawful for the company to register a transfer of shares unless a proper instrument of transfer has been furnished to the company. This is to ensure that the requisite stamp duty has been paid on foot of the transfer.

In certain situations, a shareholder may be compelled to transfer their shares. Section 204 of the 1963 Act provides that where a company acquires more than 80 per cent of the shares in another company in a take-over bid that they can compel the remaining shareholders to sell their shares at the bid price. These extensive powers are however subject to strict review by the High Court.

8.6.7 *Transmission of shares*

On the death of a shareholder his shares are vested in his personal representative and the company will, under section 81(2) of the 1963 Act, register the transfer of shares to that individual, because this happens as a matter of law. The personal representative may not wish to be registered as a member and should therefore immediately transfer the shares to the person beneficially entitled or sell them in exercise of his power as personal representative. Shares can also be transmitted by operation of law when a shareholder becomes bankrupt. Section 44(1) of the Bankruptcy Act 1988 provides that all of the bankrupt's property vests in the assignee, who can then be registered as a member. The official assignee could alternatively transfer the shares or he could seek the leave of the court to disclaim the shares after 12 months, if they are deemed to be onerous.

9. COMPANY MEETINGS

The company meeting is the vehicle through which the members and shareholders of the company can exercise their control over the company's activities. In these meetings, the individual members can exercise their right to vote and shape the decisions which are to be taken by the company. It therefore follows that the will of the company is decided by the vote of the majority of the company in the general meeting. The Companies Acts provide a legal framework for the regulation and holding of general meetings and the model articles set out the necessary technical details which are generally adopted by the majority of private companies, with certain amendments specific to the individual company. The main details relate to notice periods for meetings, the types of resolutions required to sanction action and the quorum for the meeting being present.

9.1   Types of meetings

The company can hold three types of meetings – the *annual general meeting* (A.G.M.), the *extraordinary general meeting* (E.G.M.) and the *separate meetings for certain classes* of shareholders, *e.g.* preference shareholders, where they are being asked to vote on the varying of their rights (see Chapter 8).

9.1.1   The Annual General Meeting
Section 131(1) of the 1963 Act requires that a company must hold a meeting every year as its annual general meeting, in addition to any other meetings held that year and notice of that meeting must specify that it is the annual general meeting. Section 131(2) states that a company must hold its first A.G.M. within 18 months of incorporation. If a company fail to hold an A.G.M., it is open to a member of the company to apply to the Minister under section 131(3) to order the holding of such a meeting. A single member company is given the discretion under regulation 8(1) of the (Single Member Private Limited Companies) Regulations 1994 to dispense with the holding of an AGM. The members must be given 21 days notice of the holding of the AGM and must be furnished with copies of the relevant documents. The Companies Acts require that the balance sheet, up-to-date profit and loss account, auditors' report and directors' report be placed before the meeting for inspection. However, the company articles may also state that dividends may be declared, directors may be elected and

auditors' remuneration may be dealt with at the A.G.M. If the company applies Article 53 of the model articles, then all of this business is deemed to be "ordinary business" and anything else will be "special business". It would be open to the individual member to raise other matters at the meeting. However, great emphasis is put on the giving of notice of all matters which are to be dealt with.

9.1.2 The Extraordinary General Meeting

The extraordinary general meeting is a general meeting other than the A.G.M. and not less than seven days' notice must be given for the holding of such a meeting. Under section 40 of the Companies (Amendment) Act 1983, the directors must call an E.G.M. where the company suffers a serious loss of capital, but it is also open to the members who hold not less than 10 per cent of the paid up capital which carries voting rights, to requisition the directors to call an E.G.M. by virtue of section 132 of the 1963 Act.

This gives the members an important power to compel the directors to hold a meeting where circumstances require it and cannot be varied by the articles of any company. If the directors do not convene the meeting within 21 days of this request, then the members who requisitioned may call the meeting themselves.

9.2 Notice of meetings

The Companies Acts prescribe the relevant notice periods for the holding of the various meetings, *i.e.* 21 days for an A.G.M. and seven days for an E.G.M., but it is open to the individual company in its articles to set out more extensive notice periods. The giving of notice is essential to protect the individual right of the member to attend at the meeting and to vote. Under section 136 of the 1963 Act, a member can appoint a proxy to vote in his place and that proxy need not be a member of the company. If the company fails to state in the notice that it is open to the member to appoint a proxy, then every member of the company could be open to a fine of £250 (section 15, Companies (Amendment) Act 1983). The articles of the company will usually provide (as in model Article 52) that accidental omission to give notice or the non-receipt of notice shall not invalidate a meeting, but this would be subject to the scrutiny of the courts if the individual member could prove that the omission was intentional. This is an example of the individual right of the member provided to him through the contract being breached. If business, other than the ordinary business, is to be carried on at an A.G.M., notice of this business must be given and, in the case of an E.G.M., full particulars of the business must be given to the members beforehand so that they have an opportunity to examine the matters. In *Jackson v. Munster Bank* ((1884) 13 L.R. (Ir.) 118) an injunction was granted restraining the holding of an E.G.M. where insufficient particulars regarding the business to be conducted were furnished.

9.3 Resolutions and voting at the meetings

9.3.1 *Resolutions*

For a company decision to be made on a certain matter it is necessary that the members vote, and, as has been stated above, the will of the majority will decide the company's course of action. It is open to the company in their articles to require different types of majority votes for different types of decisions and the Companies Acts will also set out instances where it is compulsory that a special majority vote is given on a matter as opposed to a simple majority vote. *Ordinary resolutions* require a simple majority vote, whereas *special resolutions* require a 75 per cent majority vote and seek to ensure that the vast majority of the company is happy with the course of action. Section 141(1) of the 1963 Act requires that 21 days notice be given of the intention to propose this form of resolution at a meeting. Special resolutions include the amending of the memorandum or articles and also the removal of a life director. Section 143 of the 1963 Act requires that all special resolutions passed by a company be registered in the Companies Office within 15 days in order to make such resolutions public knowledge. The Companies Acts also provide that there are certain matters which are dealt with by ordinary resolution but which require extended notice periods to be given, *e.g.* resolutions under section 182 of the 1963 Act, seeking to remove a director from office require that at least 28 days notice be given to the members.

9.3.2 *Voting*

The basic manner in which the will of the members is ascertained at the meeting is by a show of hands, whereby each person will have a vote and whereby the proxy could vote on behalf of a member. However, this does not take into account the varied shareholdings which members may have and therefore section 137 of the 1963 Act provides that the members may demand a poll on any resolution, thereby recognising the varying shareholdings which members may hold, as the poll will allow one vote for every share held. It is open to the individual company in their articles to provide that a vote will *always* be taken by a poll and it is not possible to exclude the right to demand a poll from a company's articles. In R *v. Lambeth* ((1839) 8 Ad. & El. 356), the poll was invalidated as a member who was entitled to vote was excluded. It is the case in certain companies that certain shares are non-voting shares and do not give the member the right to vote at meetings. The existence of such shares is frowned upon by the Stock Exchange as it is felt that persons have invested in a company but have no control over its fate. *Pender v. Lushington* ((1877) 6 Ch. D 70) is authority for the rule that only those persons listed on the register can vote, and in the case of *Kinsella v. Alliance & Dublin Gas Consumer's Company* (unreported, High Court, October 5, 1982) persons were re-fused the right to vote where their names were not on the register at the time of the vote. Transfers had been made to these individuals and their names had not yet been put on the register due to the vol-ume of transfers. Some commentators feel, that in this case, the chair-man should have used his power to adjourn the meeting because of this irregularity, but the court simply followed the rule that the register is conclusive evidence of the existence of members.

9.4   The quorum

In order that a meeting be validly constituted, it has been generally held that there must be two people present. Section 134(c) of the 1963 Act provides that two members personally present will consti-tute a quorum in a private company and this will apply unless the articles of the company require a higher quorum. If a company states in its articles that the quorum must be personally present, then a proxy cannot be taken into account. If a quorum is not present when the meeting is to begin, it must be adjourned. The articles of a company will generally provide for the appointment of a chairman to chair the meetings and that he can be appointed by the directors (Article 104, model articles). The chairman must conduct the meeting fairly and ensure that all get an opportunity to speak. The articles could state that the chairman may adjourn a meeting and that would allow him discretion, whereas the articles might state that he can only adjourn the meeting with the consent of the meeting. In *Kinsella v. Alliance & Dublin Gas Consumer's Company*, (unreported, High Court, October 5, 1982), Barron J. held that the chairman had no authority to adjourn a meeting contrary to the wishes of the majority. The chairman will propose the resolutions and will also deal with amendments to ordinary resolutions, *i.e.* a minor amendment which does not affect the substance of a resolution can be made at the meeting. Amendments cannot be made in any way to a special resolution, because parties have had to examine the way in which they will vote on the matter and things cannot then be altered at the last minute. Section 145 of the 1963 Act requires that minutes be kept of all company meetings and that they be kept at the registered office for inspection by the members. There are penalties for failure to comply with this requirement.

10. THE PROTECTION OF MINORITY SHAREHOLDERS

In Chapter 8 we examined the individual rights which are given to members by virtue of their membership of the company. Through the articles, the member is given the right to attend meetings, the right to receive a dividend when one is declared and the right to participate in the distribution of assets when the company is to be wound up. These are personal rights which the individual member can exercise and if they are breached the member can take action against the company. In *Pender v. Lushington* ((1877) 6 Ch. D. 70), it was stated that the individual member had a right to vote and that failure to allow him exercise that vote entitled the member to sue. The member will also be given other individual rights in statute, *e.g.* the right to petition for the winding up of the company and the right to receive the reports and accounts of the company.

10.1   Majority rule

However, when an individual becomes a member of a company, the contract which he enters with the company also requires that he accept as binding the decisions which are made by the majority of the company in general meeting. *Prima facie*, the company can only act through the majority voting on a particular course of action, whether that be a simple majority or a special majority vote. Therefore, the member must accept that whilst he has an interest in the company, the will of the company can only be exercised by the majority vote. The individual member may not agree with certain decisions of the majority, but if they are validly and properly made, the member has no right to take any form of action, *e.g.* the company may decide to raise capital, which could have an effect on the amount of the dividend which is to be paid out to the member, but that is not something which he can take issue with, as the company (majority) has validly decided on this course of action and the consequences are not at issue.

10.2   The rule in *Foss v. Harbottle*

Cases arose, however, where individual shareholders sought to take action where they were stating that the actions of the majority were damaging the interests of the company. In the case of *Foss v. Harbottle* ((1883) 2 Hare 461), the courts set down the rule which reflects the concept of majority rule: if a wrong was done to the company, then the proper plaintiff in that action would be the company itself, not an individual shareholder. Obviously the company would only be taking proceedings where the majority had voted to take such action. The rationale of the rule which became known as the rule in *Foss v. Harbottle* was to prevent a multiplicity of actions by disgruntled members who claimed that there were wrongs done to the company. The rule also recognised that if a wrong was done to the company, which was *intra vires* the company's capacity, then that wrong could be ratified at the general meeting by the majority and there would not then be any wrong for an individual to take issue with. In the instant case, two shareholders sought to take action against directors who they believed were carrying on acts of detriment to the company, yet the majority of the members in general meeting had refused by vote to take action against the directors. The courts said that that was the end of the matter.

A recent example of the rule being applied was in the case of *O'Neill v. Ryan* ([1990] I.L.R.M. 140). The plaintiff was the chief executive and minority shareholder of Ryanair and he was alleging that a conspiracy had been entered into by Mr Ryan, the principal shareholder of Ryanair, with Aer Lingus, which was actually detrimental to Ryanair as a company. The court refused to hear the case, saying that it was a classic example of the rule in *Foss v. Harbottle*. If the company (Ryanair) had been injured by the alleged activity of the shareholder, it was for the company as a whole, and not an individual member to take an action. O'Neill was claiming that the value of his shareholding in the company had been reduced as a result of the transactions, yet this was one of the matters with which an individual member cannot take issue. Lynch J said: "the desirability of avoiding a multiplicity of actions perhaps in many cases contrary to the will of directors and/or majority of shareholders is obviously a major factor in the thinking underlying the rule".

10.3   Exceptions to the rule in *Foss v. Harbottle*

The difficulty with the rule in *Foss v. Harbottle*, however, is that it presumes that the majority have the power to ratify the wrong in question *and* that the majority have the company's interests at heart, in that their interests and those of the company are mutually inclusive. This, however, is not always the case and so there must be exceptions to the rule, so that all eventualities are catered for. Four exceptions have been established at common law to the rule in *Foss v. Harbottle* which would otherwise preclude the member from ever taking action:

(i) The member has never been prevented from taking action when one of the *individual membership rights* has been breached. Indeed this is not necessarily an exception to the rule, as the right to take action on foot of these breaches was established in *Pender v. Lushington* ((1877) 6 Ch. D. 70) and is not questioned. In *Hennessy v. National Agricultural Association* ([1947] I.R. 159), the plaintiff successfully brought a personal action where the quorum in general meeting had not been observed.

(ii) The member is given the right to take action where the *requisite majority required for the passing of a vote is not reached* and the company purports to act on the strength of that lesser vote, *e.g.* if the 75 per cent majority required for the alteration of the objects clause was not reached and the company purports to alter regardless, then the individual member is given the right to sue. The reasoning here is that the majority are sanctioning this wrongdoing and will certainly not seek to take action to redress it, so the individual is given the right.

(iii) The member is also given the right to take action on foot of an *ultra vires* action. The majority cannot commit an act which is *ultra vires* the company. Section 8(2) of the 1963 Act provides that any member can bring an action to prevent a company doing an act which is *ultra vires*, or beyond its capacity. The rationale is that the majority are acting outside the interests of the company so the principle of majority rule has been nullified and the minority must be allowed to take action on behalf of the company. In *Simpson v. Westminster Palace Hotels Co.* ((1860) 10 H.L. 712), a member was permitted to take action to have the *ultra vires* transaction set aside and was also permitted to seek recovery of money which the company had wrongfully transferred on foot of the transaction. The rationale behind this rule is that the individual member should be allowed to take an action on behalf of the company, as otherwise the wrong will go unredressed and the company cannot

ratify the *ultra vires* act. There have been decisions in
England which suggest that the individual member may
not be permitted to take action on foot of an *ultra vires*
act which has already been carried out where a substantial number of independent shareholders are against
the case being heard because of the damage which the
litigation could bring on the company, *Smith v. Croft
(No.2)* ([1988] Ch. 114). This reasoning has been felt to
be unconvincing in an Irish context.

(iv) The member is also permitted to take an action where
it is alleged that the majority in control have perpetrated, or attempted to commit a *"fraud on the minority"*.
The term "fraud" is defined widely and will include all
forms of conduct which are deemed to be inequitable.
This exception arises where the majority of the shareholders are using the powers entrusted to them for
motives other than for the *best interests of the company*.
The member can take what is known as a "derivative
action" which is taken on behalf of the company to
right the wrong done to the company. It is clear that
the action can only be brought where there is a wrongful, fraudulent motive apparent in the actions of the
majority. In *Greenhalgh v. Arderne Cinemas Ltd.* ([1951]
Ch. 286), the plaintiff shareholder was not successful
in his action where he claimed that the majority had
altered the articles to exclude the right of pre-emption,
and that that was detrimental to him. There was nothing inherently wrong with that decision and no ulterior
motives were found. Most of the cases that have been
brought under this exception either involve the majority expropriating the company property in some way or
by diverting opportunities, which were open to the company, to themselves.

In *Cook v. Deeks* ([1916] 1 A.C. 554), director/shareholders of a company had used information available to them by virtue of their position to divert a contract from the company to themselves personally,
and had used their majority vote to pass a special resolution sanctioning this action. The minority shareholders were able to have the transaction set aside as it was a fraud on the minority. Other transactions

may not be so obviously wrong, but may still be set aside as a *fraud on the minority* because the majority are not acting in the best interests of the company. In *Parke v. Daily News* ([1961] 1 All E.R. 695), the majority shareholders were selling their interests in the newspapers and sought to distribute the proceeds of sale of these main assets amongst the employees of the newspapers who would then be redundant. The individual shareholder took an action on the grounds that this was not in the best interests of the company and that it was not authorised by the memorandum, and thus restrained them from carrying out this transaction. In *Nash v. Lancegaye Safety Glass (Ireland) Ltd* ((1958) 92 I.L.T.R. 11) the plaintiff was a director/shareholder in the defendant company and claimed that there had been a fraud on the minority when the majority had sanctioned a new allotment of preference shares to an individual in order to increase the voting power within the company. He had called an extraordinary general meeting to deal with this issue, as he had over 10 per cent of the shareholding, but then issued proceedings as he realised that the increased number of votes would then be weighted against him in any vote. The court agreed that the allotment of shares had been an improper use by the directors of their powers.

It is important for an individual member to take all steps open to him before issuing proceedings, *e.g.* in the above case the member called the E.G.M. to get the company to vote on the validity of the allotment but then had to take proceedings because he realised that the majority wrong was already in being. A hasty member could find, after issuing proceedings, that there was enough of a majority within the company to set aside the transaction which had actually only been sanctioned by a group of directors.

Some commentators have stated that there may be a fifth exception to the rule in *Foss v. Harbottle* and that the courts will allow members take claims where this is in the interests of justice. However, this thinking has derived from *obiter* remarks in cases where the claim was allowed within one of the other exceptions. It is felt that the exceptions are interpreted widely enough to permit all worthy claims.

10.4   Section 205 of the Companies Act 1963

If a minority shareholder could not fit within the requirements of one of the exceptions to the rule in *Foss v. Harbottle*, his only means of doing something about the alleged wrong was to seek that the court wind up the company because it was just and equitable that the court do this. This, however, was not a real alternative as it could mean assets being sold off at an undervalue. The legislature therefore saw fit to introduce a statutory vehicle through which shareholders could bring action. Section 205 of the Companies Act 1963 provides that any member of a company who complains that its affairs are being conducted in a manner oppressive to him or any of the members, or in disregard of his or their interests as members, or that the directors' powers are being exercised in a similar manner, can apply to the court for an order to remedy that state of affairs. If the court accepts the claim, it can make a number of different orders. They could cancel the impugned transaction or direct that certain actions be taken. The court can also order that the shares of the applicant who complains of the wrong be bought by the majority at a favourable price, as it is not practical to expect these parties to continue in the same company. The court could also order that the minority shareholders purchase the shares of the majority. If there is no hope for the existence of the company as a result of the actions, then the court can use its powers under section 213(f) of the 1963 Act to wind up the company as it is just and equitable to do this. Under the common law exceptions, the court would only be in a position to set aside the impugned transaction, therefore section 205 had a wealth of remedies. There are few reported decisions on the use of the statutory provision in Ireland, but it is felt that most of the cases which concern a section 205 petition are settled before the court has to decide upon them.

10.4.1 *Who can claim relief under section 205?*
It has been stated that a claimant need not be in the minority to avail of section 205 and that it is open to a majority group of shareholders to take a claim under the section to seek a court remedy because they are being oppressed or their rights are being disregarded.

The section requires that, in order to establish a claim, the affairs of the company must be carried out in a manner which is oppressive to the members or in disregard of their interests *as members*. In England it has been made clear in the 1985 Companies Act that the oppression of the individual need not be in his capacity as a member, but it could include oppression in his capacity as a director. This is of relevance, as in most small private companies, the shareholders will be directors and the particular form of oppression may attack them primarily as directors. This has not been specifically written into Irish legislation but in the case of Re *Murph's Restaurant Ltd.* ([1979] I.L.R.M.

141), the courts agreed that an attempt by the majority to oust a fellow member director from a small partnership type company which was based on mutual trust and understanding constituted oppression and did not dwell on the fact that the oppression was suffered in the individual's capacity as director. In that case, the courts felt that the only remedy which could be offered was to wind the company up under section 213(f) on just and equitable grounds, as the whole sub-stratum of the company had been eroded.

However, the second limb of the section requires that there be disregard of the interests of the individual in their *capacity as member* and this would therefore exclude the director from claiming for disregard of interests.

10.4.2   *What is oppressive conduct ?*

The most often cited definition of oppression is that given by Lord Simonds in *Scottish CWS Ltd. v. Meyer* ([1959] A.C. 324) which is approved by Keane J. in *Re Greenore Trading Co.* ([1980] I.L.R.M. 94), where he said that oppression is any conduct which is "burdensome, harsh and wrongful". In *Re Jermyn Street Turkish Baths Ltd.* ([1971] 3 All E.R. 184), it was stated that oppression connoted some lack of probity or fair dealing towards one or more members of the company and need not be something illegal. In *Re Greenore Trading* ([1980] I.L.R.M. 94), an action was taken on foot of section 205 claiming that there had been oppression. There were three shareholders in the company each initially holding one-third of the shares. B decided to leave and agreed to sell his shares to V for a sum. V only paid part of the sum, with the company resources paying the remainder. It was claimed by the defendants that the company payout to B was like a compensation payment to him for leaving, but P, the petitioner, came before the court claiming oppression and the court accepted that. The court said that the payment should have been disclosed to, and approved by, the general meeting under section 186 of the 1963 Act, or in the alternative, it was a payment which constituted the provision of financial assistance by the company for the purchase of its own shares and was therefore in breach of section 60 of the 1963 Act. The applicant could have sought relief under the common law exceptions but that did not prevent him from taking action here. In *Crindle Investments v. Wymes* ([1998] 4 I.R. 567), the applicants were successful in a section 205 application. The case concerned litigation which had been ongoing for some time. Two of the four shareholders of the company had agreed to settlement proposals put by the other side, but the other two refused to accept them. The applicants claimed that the conduct of the majority in rejecting the offer was so unreasonable as to constitute oppression. The courts agreed with this. The case of *Re Westwinds Holdings* (unreported, High Court, Kenny J., May 1974) is authority for the proposition that a single wrongful act can amount to oppression, and that there is no need for a course of misconduct. The question of whether oppression has occurred is an objective test and the conduct which may be assessed as oppressive will depend on all the circumstances of the case.

10.5　Disregard of interests

The disregard of interests must be in the applicant's capacity as a member. In *Re Williams Group (Tullamore) Ltd.* ([1986] I.R. 217), the court held that there had been disregard of the interests of the members. The ordinary shareholders did not have the right to vote as this was exclusive to the preference shareholders. The ordinary shareholders had always had the variable dividends payable to them, and the preference shareholders had a fixed rate dividend paid. However, windfall profits had come in, and the preference shareholders sought to issue a new class of shares rearranging the payment of this profit in order to benefit themselves. The court held that this was being done in disregard of the interests of the other shareholders. Many commentators do not see a huge difference between oppression and disregard of interests.

In *McCormack v. Cameo Investments* (unreported, October 1978), and in *Re Clubman Shirts* ([1983] I.L.R.M. 323), it was felt that negligence, carelessness and irregularity alone would not constitute oppression. Just because a director can claim to act honestly and in good faith does not mean they will escape liability under section 205 as the conduct is objectively assessed, therefore the section 205 action is better than the common law exceptions.

10.6　*"In camera"* proceedings

In the past, it was a matter of course that applications for the hearing of these actions to be *in camera* would be granted. However, in *Re R Ltd.* ([1989] I.L.R.M. 757), the Supreme Court stated that whilst *some* of the matters which concerned areas of a sensitive commercial nature may be heard *in camera*, the case should otherwise be heard in public.

In *Irish Press v Ingersoll Ltd.* ([1994] 1 I.R. 176), the Supreme Court said that all section 205 applications would be heard in public unless:

(i)   a public hearing would involve the disclosure of information which would be prejudicial to the company; and

(ii) would fall short of doing justice, however, it was clarified that to show this, one would have to show a great prejudice.

There is therefore a high threshold of requirements before the court would accede to the request to have the matter dealt with *in camera*. This is felt to reflect the fact that companies are given certain rights at incorporation but that transparency of dealings should always be to the fore, and there is no exception when the matters go to litigation.

11. THE MANAGEMENT OF THE COMPANY

11.1 The division of powers between the members and the directors

The Companies Acts 1963–99 require that certain major decisions of the company must be taken by the members sitting in general meeting. Section 10 of the Companies Act 1963 requires a 75 per cent majority vote of the members before the objects clause can be altered whilst other sections require that the company must decide in general meeting whether to issue new shares or waive pre-emption rights. Apart from these powers which *must* be exercised by the members in general meeting, it is open to the members in a company to delegate power to the board of directors who will carry on the day-to-day management of the company. If some power is not delegated to the directors, then that power will automatically fall to be decided by the members in general meeting. Effectively, the allocation of power in any private company will depend on the particular articles and regulations of the company and may even be supplemented by separate contractual arrangements.

Certain model articles would delegate *specific* powers to the directors and can be included in the company's articles of association, *e.g.* Article 79 provides that the directors can borrow money and give security on behalf of the company, whilst Article 5 provides that the directors of the company can allot unissued shares (within the authorisation limit set by the members in general meeting). Article 15 provides that the directors can make calls on shares from time to time. However, Article 80 of the model articles of association is a very general authority and, if included in the articles of a company, would empower the board to "manage the business of the company", and "to exercise all such powers of the company" which are not required to be exercised by the company in general meeting, whilst at the same time accepting "directions" from the general meeting. This effectively gives the board managerial autonomy to make *all* necessary decisions. It is believed that the general meeting cannot interfere with the autonomy of the board once this power has been given over, other than by altering the articles in general meeting or by removing the existing directors by an ordinary resolution in general meeting.

So what type of business will the Article 80 clause transfer to the directors? There would appear to be three categories of business decisions:

(i)   It has been accepted as a matter of course that, if an Article 80-type clause is employed, the directors will have the power to carry on the *everyday tasks* of business, *e.g.* hiring employees, selecting suppliers and contracting with buyers and that the members would not be permitted to veto these decisions in any way, as they have transferred such authority. In *Scott v. Scott* ([1943] 1 All E.R. 582), the members in general meeting attempted to dictate dividend policy to the board. The court held that this was an ordinary financial matter which was purely a matter for the management of the business and that the members in general meeting could have no say in the matter because such authority had been delegated to the board by virtue of an Article 80-type provision.

(ii) The case of *Automatic Self Cleansing Filter v. Cunninghame* ([1906] 2 Ch. 34) is authority for the proposition that, if an Article 80-type clause is included in the articles of association, the directors will have the authority to make *major management decisions*, *e.g.* the sale of major assets, expansions and takeovers. The members will not be in a position to veto the decision, as they have originally transferred the authority. These types of decisions are distinguished from "structural decisions", *e.g.* altering objects or repaying capital which by law require the consent of the general meeting. In the above case, the members sought to instruct the board to sell the company's undertaking and, by virtue of the transfer of power, it was felt that they could not do this. The court spoke of the presumption of board autonomy, that in the absence of any indication to the contrary: "it is not competent for the majority of shareholders at a general meeting to affect or alter the mandate originally given to the directors by the articles."

(iii) The case of *Breckland Group Holdings v. London & Suffolk Properties Ltd.* ([1989] B.C.L.C. 100) is authority for the proposition that if an Article 80-type clause is included in the articles of association then only the directors can *commence proceedings* in the company name, as this is felt to be within the business of the company.

In that case, the majority shareholder commenced an action in the company name as against another company, with no reference to the directors. Harman J. said that the conduct of business had been passed to the directors and the members could not then intervene. He said that the action had been wrongly brought by the member and if the board did not adopt the decision to act, then the general meeting would have no power to override the decision of the board. Nothing in the above would, however, permit the directors from preventing a derivative action being brought by the minority who are claiming that the majority or the directors have perpetrated fraud.

In conclusion, it is clear that when the members devolve power to the directors they waive their rights to control that particular area of decision-making. Of course, in many companies certain specific areas of decision-making, over and above that required by law, will be left with the general meeting.

Regardless of an Article 80-type provision being in place, power can revert to the members in certain instances:

(i)   Power will always revert to the members in default. Therefore, where the directors resign or die, the members will have the power in default, *e.g.* in *Mahony v. East Holyford Mining Co.* ((1875) L.R. 7 H.L. 869) where it was held that where there was no official board of directors, the members of the company had the power to hold out certain of their number as being directors.

(ii) Power will also revert to the members where the directors exceed their delegated authority. An example of this is *Re Burke Clancy & Co. Ltd.* (unreported, High Court, May 23, 1974). In that case, the directors of the company purported to borrow more money than they were authorised to do under the articles of association. However, the members approved the transaction in the general meeting and Kenny J. spoke of how "it was established law that the members of a company may ratify acts which are outside the powers of directors but are *intra vires* the company". The rationale is that the members can validate unauthorised acts of the directors which are *intra vires* the company's capacity because the directors' powers derive from the members. The members could not ratify the acts of the directors which are *ultra vires* the company's capacity.

(iii) Where the board is deadlocked and cannot reach a decision on some matter within its competence then the matter will fall to be decided by the members in general meeting.

(iv) The members can effectively divert power back to themselves, even though they have originally delegated the powers of management to the directors, by amending the articles of association by special resolution under section 15 of the 1963 Act, and thereby regain the power to manage the company's business. The fact that the directors know that this power exists will encourage them to act according to the wishes of the members.

11.2   The directors

The directors of a company are generally vested with the everyday control of the company and will act on behalf of the members of the company pursuant to Article 80 of the model articles of association. Article 110 then provides that the board can appoint a managing director from amongst their number, and under Article 112 they will confer on him the powers which they see fit. The directors stand in a fiduciary position to the company and have a duty to act in good faith in the interest of the company as a whole. As fiduciaries, the directors cannot retain benefits that they have acquired as a result of their position as directors with the company. Directors are required to make full disclosure to the company of all such matters. Directors may be either executive or non-executive directors with the former being a full-time employee of the company with a salary, and the latter simply receiving directors' fees if this has been provided by the general meeting. The law deems that both owe the same duties to the company. Section 27 of the Companies Act 1990 places all of these requirements on *shadow directors* also. A shadow director is defined as: "a person in accordance with whose directions or instructions the directors of a company are accustomed to act". (The duties of the director will be examined in Chapter 12.)

The first directors of a company must be named in the statement furnished to the Registrar pursuant to section 3 of the 1982 Act, and the first directors will also be named in the articles of association of the company. Section 174 of the Companies Act 1963 requires that all companies must have two directors, yet this is somewhat anomalous now, given that, since 1994, a private company can consist of one member. The articles of association of the particular company should then provide for the appointment and retirement of directors. Section 43 of the Companies (Amendment) (No. 2) Act 1999 introduces a new restriction in relation to the parties who may act as a director of a company by requiring that at least one director must be resident in the State. This requirement has been introduced due to concerns that directors who were not resident within the State could not be prosecuted for breaches of company legislation. A company can circumvent the requirement if they enter a £20,000 bond securing the payment of any fine that would be imposed. Section 45 of the Companies (Amendment) (No.2) Act 1999 also sets out that a person cannot hold more than 25 directorships of different companies at any one time. This provision seeks to limit the formation of companies that have no link with the State. Section 195 of the Companies Act 1963 required the company to keep a register of directors and secretaries, and section 51 of the Companies Act 1990 added a further requirement to notify the Registrar within 14 days of any change in directors. Under section 53 of the Companies Act 1990 the company must keep a register of director's shareholdings within the company, and the directors and secretaries must make disclosure to the company of their interests in the shares and any dealings which they have entered into in relation to the shares.

11.3   The company secretary

Every company must have a secretary who may well be one of the directors. The secretary can be named in the memorandum or articles of association or can be appointed by the members in general meeting, or by the directors. The name of the secretary must be furnished to the Registrar under section 3 of the Companies Act 1982. The secretary carries out a mainly administrative function within the company and is responsible for such things as: making the annual returns, giving notice to members of meetings and notifying the Registrar of any changes in the company documentation.

In some larger companies, the secretary could be a firm of accountants or financial consultants. The secretary may be expressly authorised to enter into a specific transaction on behalf of the company or may have the apparent authority to enter into a specific contract in the role of secretary, but these will generally be administrative-type matters and a secretary would not have apparent authority to enter any form of commercial contract on behalf of the company as this would not be within the role of a secretary.

11.4   Appointment of directors

After formation, it may be necessary to appoint further directors, and if the articles do not provide for such appointment, then the directors must be appointed by the members in general meeting. Section 181 of the Companies Act 1963 provides that it is not possible to propose the election of a board of directors by a single resolution, unless all of the members present at the meeting agree to this. This seeks to prevent an automatic "board" of candidates being placed before the members and requires that each be proposed individually. If the articles of association state that the board can then appoint further directors, the members can have no say in these appointments, unless they amend the articles by special resolution in general meeting. The articles will usually provide that the directors can fill casual vacancies. It is clear that a director need not own any shares in a company, but often the articles will provide that the directors must own a certain number of shares and if this is the case, section 180 of the Companies Act 1963 requires that the director obtain the shares within two months of his appointment. The articles would also usually provide for the vacation of office by a director if he becomes of unsound mind, resigns, is convicted of an indictable offence or is absent from meetings for six months without permission.

11.5   Dismissal of directors

It is a basic principle of company law that the members of a company can dismiss or remove a director by passing an ordinary resolution in a general meeting. This right is furnished to the members by section 182 of the Companies Act 1963 and cannot be removed by the articles of a particular company. It is provided, however, in subsection (1) that a director appointed for life in a private company cannot be removed by ordinary resolution. Such a director could only be dismissed if a special *resolution* altering the articles was passed. The director must be given 28 days' notice of the proposed resolution to dismiss him and he can be heard at the meeting. Where the resolution of the members is invalid or the director is deprived of his statutory rights to notice, he may seek an injunction declaring that his removal was invalid. In *Coubrough v. James Panton & Co. Ltd.* ([1965] I.R. 272), an ordinary resolution was passed instead of a special resolution (as required under that company's articles and accordingly was invalid).

It is important to note that each company can adopt its own articles. After all, it is the members who are deciding. If the other directors decide to expel one of their number from the board, they must exercise this power bona fide and in the interests of the company and not for ulterior purposes (*Lee v. Chou Wen Hsien et al* ([1985] B.C.L.C. 45)).

Although the company acting through its members has the power to dismiss a director by virtue of the Companies Act 1963, certain factors may deter them from this course of action. Obviously the matter of labour law remedies will exist, so while section 182(1) sets out the statutory power to dismiss, section 182(7) provides that the right to compensation or damages payable to the director, remains intact. To have rights against the company, the director must have been employed on a contractual basis as opposed to merely being appointed by resolution. Where there is a service contract, express or implied, and the director is dismissed in contravention or in breach of the Unfair Dismissals Acts 1977–93 or wrongfully dismissed, then his right to compensation may be invoked. The director will also be able to rely on the principles of natural justice if the requisite notice periods or procedural matters are not complied with in dismissing the director (*Glover v. B.L.N.* ([1973] I.R. 388)). Section 50 of the Companies Act 1990 requires that every service contract with every director be kept in the registered office so that shareholders can inspect same.

Also, it may be possible for the director who is being dismissed to take a section 205 application claiming that he is being oppressed as a director or that his rights as a member are being disregarded. In *McGilligan v. O'Grady* ([1999] 1 I.R. 346), the plaintiff director was successful in obtaining injunctive relief restraining the defendants from dismissing him as their conduct was deemed to be oppressive. The Supreme Court upheld the High Court saying that the essence of a section 205 application was to allow relief from the actions of the majority, even if those actions were lawful.

11.6   Remuneration of directors

Whilst a director has no particular right to be remunerated for acting as a director, Article 76 of the model articles of association provides that the members in general meeting can decide on the remuneration of directors and can also provide the director with an expense account. *Harvey Lewis's Case* ((1872) 26 L.T. 673) stated that the amount of remuneration was at the discretion of the general meeting and that it did not have to be paid out of profits. However, in *Re Holt Garage (1964) Ltd.* ([1982] 3 All E.R. 1016), it was stated that if the remuneration was excessive and was not authorised by the company in general meeting, or if it was really a return of capital, it would be unlawful. If the director accepts remuneration in excess of what he has been voted, he is guilty of misfeasance and the excess can be reclaimed from him by the company or the liquidator. Section 191 of the Companies Act 1963 requires that directors' salaries be set out in the annual accounts which are laid before the annual general meeting.

11.7   Loans to directors

Section 31 of the Companies Act 1990 prohibits the making of loans by the company to directors and also covers a wide range of related transactions. Prior to the introduction of the 1990 Act, it may have been possible for the director to obtain a loan from the company, which in many cases was irrecoverable, and was therefore detrimental to the creditors of the company. The section provides that a company cannot make a loan to a director of the company or of its holding company. The section also prohibits:

- *quasi loans* - whereby the company could agree to reimburse expenditure of the director;
- *credit transactions* - whereby the company could be paying the directors' liability on a hire purchase agreement; and
- the giving of *guarantees* by the company for a director's loan.

The restriction also applies to shadow directors and persons connected with directors, *e.g.* spouses, partners, etc. Section 31(2) prevents the company taking over a transaction which, if originally entered into by it, would have been in breach of section 31. Section 31(3) also prevents the company becoming involved in a transaction whereby someone else makes the loan to the director and gets some form of benefit from the company.

However, there are exemptions to the rule. Exemption is created where the amount at issue is relatively small, *i.e.* less than 10 per cent of the company's relevant (net) assets. However, if the sum is not quantifiable, then it will be taken to be in excess of that amount and will be prohibited. Section 34 allows an exemption where loans are made between holding companies and subsidiary companies, whereby directors may be involved in one or other of the companies. Section 36 allows a director to be advanced money for expenses. Section 37 also allows an exemption whereby the company makes loans, guarantees etc. in the ordinary course of its business.

If these transactions are entered into contrary to the Companies Acts, the transaction is voidable at the instance of the company. If the company is wound up and it is believed that the loan given contributed materially to the insolvency, then the person to whom the loan was given can be made personally liable for the debts of the company, with or without limitation.

11.8   Miscellaneous transactions with directors

Various other sections in the 1990 Act impose restrictions on the directors in cases where the directors could receive benefits to the detriment of the other shareholders and creditors. Section 29(1) provides that if a director acquires substantial property from the company or vice versa, the transaction must be approved by the company in general meeting. In order to come within this restriction, the property must have a value in excess of 10 per cent of the company's net assets. The company can avoid such a transaction and can require the director to account to the company for any profit made by him. Section 30 of the 1990 Act now absolutely prohibits directors from buying options in the shares or debentures in the company. This would be capable of abuse as it would otherwise allow the director to use his knowledge to arrange the right to buy or sell his shares in the company at a particular time for a specified price.

11.9   Meetings of directors

The board of directors must hold meetings to make decisions in relation to the management of the company. As with the general meetings of the members, the meetings of the board must be properly convened and conducted so that any decisions made can be deemed valid. The articles of the particular company will set out the procedure in relation to the board meetings. Article 101 of the model articles of association provides that the directors "may meet together for the despatch of business, adjourn, and otherwise regulate their meetings as they think fit". The articles would also usually provide that a director can call a meeting at any time and that a quorum, generally of two members, must be present for the meeting to be valid. All directors must receive notice of the meetings, except if they are out of the State. Article 109 of the model articles of association provides that a resolution signed by all of the directors shall be valid as if it were passed at a valid convened meeting. It is noted that if some regulation within the articles is not complied with and a resolution is passed thereon, the outsider who has entered the transaction with the company can benefit from the "indoor management" rule, as they could not be aware of the board's failure to adhere to regulation.

11.10 Restriction and disqualification of directors

Directors who have been exposed, through the vehicle of a court-ordered winding up, can be restricted or disqualified from acting as directors in the future. These provisions act as a deterrent for errant directors. In a sense, they are under-used because only directors in companies that have been wound up by the courts can be so exposed. Therefore, reliance is placed on the liquidator to take the relevant actions against the directors. The provisions are of little use in a small company that has been wound up by a voluntary liquidator, where the acts or omissions of the directors will not be brought to public attention.

Part VII of the Companies Act 1990 introduced the framework whereby directors of insolvent companies which are wound up by the court could be severely restricted from acting as directors in the future, and whereby directors could be absolutely prohibited or disqualified from acting as directors for a prescribed period of time.

11.10.1 Restriction

Section 150 of the Companies Act 1990 sets out that, *prima facie*, a director who has acted as a director in a company in the 12 months prior to it being wound up (including shadow directors) can be restricted from acting as a director for a period of five years. The provisions come into effect where it is proven that the company was unable to pay its debts prior to the commencement of winding up, or where the liquidator certifies that during the course of the winding up that the company was unable to pay its debts. Therefore, the legislation seeks to expose directors who have let the company fail. However, there is a saver to this provision in section 150(2) which provides that the director will not be so restricted if he can prove to the court that he acted *"honestly and responsibly"* in relation to the company affairs and should not therefore be restricted. This allows the directors to attempt to defend their actions and in the case of *Re Costello Doors Ltd.* (unreported, High Court, July 21, 1995), the court held that the maintenance of proper books and accounts and the employment of experts to look after things "would go a long way to discharge the onus of showing that the directors behaved responsibly". In *Business Communications Ltd. v. Baxter & Parsons* (unreported, High Court, July 21, 1995), the same court refused to accept the plea that the director had acted *honestly and responsibly* and said that the decision to trade on for a period of more than six months was imprudent in the extreme. The rationale for this holding was that if the director had acted responsibly he would have voluntarily wound up the company six months earlier. In *Re Ashclad Limited* (unreported, High Court, April 5, 2000), a restriction order was granted where the directors had failed to keep proper books of account, had failed to have the accounts audited or keep any form of invoices or records of wages or VAT details. The directors were also made personally liable, under section 202 of the 1990, Act for failing to keep the proper books of account. In *Re Squash Ireland Ltd.* (unreported, February 8, 2001), the Supreme Court overturned a High Court decision to restrict the directors of the insolvent company. The court stated that a number of factors should be considered in deciding whether the directors had acted *"honestly or responsibly"*. These included the extent to which the director had failed to comply with the requirements of legislation, whether he had acted with commercial probity, whether his conduct was responsible for the insolvency, whether his conduct had resulted in the deficiency in assets at the date of winding up and whether his conduct had been so incompetent as to be irresponsible. In this case, the court felt that the directors, who had acted for 18 years within the company, had acted honestly and responsibly and should not be restricted. The court said they had to look at the directors' whole tenure in office and judge them accordingly.

Under section 150(2)(b) the courts will not restrict a director of the insolvent company who is proven to be simply a nominee director, *i.e.* someone who has been nominated to the board by a financial institution in connection with the giving of credit. Under section 150(3), certain criteria are set out whereby a director who has been generally restricted by an order will not be prevented from acting as a director of a company which has a certain level of paid up share capital. The rationale for this seems to be based on the diminishment of risk due to the healthy capital of the company. At present, a private company which the restricted director proposes to act for must have a paid up share capital of £20,000 and a public company must have a paid up share capital of £100,000. The Company Law (Enforcement) Bill 2000 proposes to increase these figures, but has not yet become law.

11.10.1.1 *Consequences of restriction*
Section 150 states that the restriction period shall run for five years and section 153 requires that a register of restricted directors be kept. However, section 152 allows the director to apply to the court for a relaxation of the restriction after one year and the court can relax the restriction if they feel that it is just and equitable to do so.

11.10.1.2 *Reform*
As noted earlier, the problem with enforcing these provisions lies in the fact that the only individual who will bring these matters to the court's attention is the liquidator. Whilst section 151 of the 1990 Act imposes a fine on a liquidator who does not draw the attention of the court to the necessary wrongdoing, it is still the case that the majority of directors involved in companies that have been wound up outside of court, will not become subject to these provisions. The Company Law (Enforcement) Bill 2000 seeks to create a new office of the Director of Corporate Enforcement. Part of the role of this office would be to monitor companies. The Director could make application to court seeking the restriction order and the challenged director would be liable for the costs of this application.

11.10.2 *Disqualification*
Section 160 of the 1990 Act provides for the prohibition of a director from acting as a director for a prescribed period of time. Section 160(1) provides that a director will be automatically disqualified from acting as a director for five years where he commits an indictable offence in relation to the company. This section also applies to an auditor, of-

ficer, receiver or examiner. However, section 160(2) gives the court discretion to disqualify a director either at their own behest or if the application is made to the court, *e.g.* the court could make a disqualification order upon hearing the facts of a section 205 application.

The grounds upon which the court can exercise their discretion to disqualify are set out in section 160(2) and include:

- where the officer has been guilty of fraud in relation to the company;
- where found guilty of a breach of duty;
- where found personally liable for the debts of a company pursuant to fraudulent or reckless trading;
- where the court feels that the individual is unfit to be concerned in the management of a company;
- where an inspector's report states that the individual is unfit to act;
- where the individual has been in persistent default in the making of returns to the Registrar.

This final reason would seem to require three or more defaults. The Company Law (Enforcement) Bill 2000 seeks to include a further ground that where a person has been found guilty under section 202(10) for failing to keep proper books of account on two occasions, he can be disqualified.

11.10.2.1 *Who can apply for an order?*
The application may be made in any civil or criminal proceedings relating to the director, *e.g.* reckless trading, and can also be made independently under section 160. The application can be made by any member, officer, creditor, examiner or liquidator of the company or by the Director of Public Prosecutions or the Registrar of Companies.

11.10.2.2 *Consequences of disqualification*
The director will be prohibited from acting as a director for a prescribed period of time and his name will be placed on the Register of disqualified directors. If the director acts as a director whilst prohibited from doing so, section 161 provides that the director is guilty of a criminal offence and is subject to prosecution summarily or on indictment. Section 163 then provides that the director who breaches

the disqualification order and acts for a company which is then wound up, shall also be personally liable for all the debts incurred by that company whilst he was so acting and the company will be able to recover any consideration paid over to him in that time. Section 164 also imposes liability on persons who act under a disqualified director, knowing him to be disqualified. They too are then disqualified and may be personally liable for debts incurred during the time they were acting.

11.10.2.3 Test for disqualification

In the case of *Business Communications Ltd. v. Baxter & Parsons* (unreported, High Court, July 21, 1995), Murphy J. said that there was a much stronger burden of proof resting on a director who was attempting to extricate himself from a disqualification order than there was to evade a restriction order. In one of the few Irish cases where a disqualification order was made, *Re Christy Kenneally Communications Ltd.* (unreported, High Court, July 1992), Costello J. imposed the order on two directors who had refused to comply with a court order to prepare annual accounts and hold an A.G.M. No defence for the directors is set out in the statute and is therefore at the discretion of the court. In England, the courts seem to use a subjective test and take such matters as age and experience into account, *Re Chartmore Limited* ([1990] B.C.L.C. 673) and *Re Cladrose* ([1990] B.C.L.C. 204). In the case of *Re Dawson Print Group* ([1987] B.C.L.C. 204), Hoffman J. stated that every case turned on its own facts and that conduct which would result in disqualification must be in breach of the standards of commercial morality.

12. THE DUTIES OF DIRECTORS

12.1 Introduction

In the previous chapter, we looked at the manner in which the company in general meeting delegates powers to the directors to act on behalf of the company. If an Article 80-type provision is present in the company articles, then the directors can exercise all of the powers of the company other than those which are specifically retained by the company in general meeting. The company cannot interfere in a decision which has been delegated to the directors and cannot set aside such a decision which has been properly taken. It was noted, however, in the previous chapter that the power still remains with the company in general meeting to amend the articles and call back the delegated power or to dismiss the directors by ordinary resolution.

The duties owed by directors and other corporate officers to their company are wide and diverse. The sources of the duties are found in *common law*, in *equity* and in *statute*. In law, a director stands in a fiduciary position to the company of which he is an officer. As a fiduciary, the director has power to deal with the property of the company, and is assumed therefore to occupy a position of trust and confidence in relation to the company which may loosely be referred to as the beneficiary. The director must act reasonably, in good faith in the interests of the company as a whole, and is not permitted to make a personal profit by virtue of his position within the company.

12.2 To whom are the duties owed?

12.2.1 The company

The general rule has always been that the directors owe their duty to the company itself, and not to the individual shareholders of the company. The directors act as agents of the company and accordingly, the duties are owed to the principal, *i.e.* the company as a whole from whom they derive power. Therefore, if a director acts in excess or breach of his powers, it is up to the company in general meeting to decide whether the particular act is to be ratified and it is up to them to decide whether action shall be taken against the director. This principle was first established in the case of *Percival v. Wright* ([1902] 2 Ch. 421). In that case, a director of the company purchased shares from a member and did not inform the member that there were negotiations in being for the purchase of all the shares at a much higher price. The member alleged that the director had been in breach of fiduciary duty and sought that he account for the profit. Swinfen Eady J. held that there was no fiduciary duty owed to the individual shareholder. The director was acting in the interests of the company as a whole. In *Dawson International plc v. Coats Paton plc* ([1989] B.C.L.C. 243), it was made clear that directors acting in the interests of the company may have to act in a manner which could be disadvantageous to individual shareholders. Lord Cullen said that what is in the interest of current shareholders who may wish to sell their shares at present, may not necessarily be in the interests of the company as a whole and accordingly "directors have but one master, the company".

However, the directors can be deemed in certain transactions to be acting on behalf of, and as agents of, the individual shareholders. This was held in the case of *Allen v. Hyatt* ((1914) 30 T.L.R) where it was felt that the directors had held themselves out as acting for specific shareholders and must therefore be deemed to owe a duty to them.

In the New Zealand case of *Coleman v. Myers* ([1977] 2 N.Z.L.R. 225), the courts found that the directors had acted in breach of fiduciary duty to the shareholders, who were members of their own families, by withholding information on the value of their shares which they were attempting to acquire. In assessing whether the special relationship is created between directors and particular shareholders as regards a particular transaction, the courts will consider whether there was:

- existence of a relationship of confidence;
- dependence upon information and advice given;
- significance of some particular transaction for the parties; and
- any positive action taken by the directors to promote it.

In the above case, it was felt that the directors had taken on a responsibility towards the shareholders and a fiduciary duty existed which was breached. The fact that the company was a small, family company added to the extent of the duty. This case was approved in Ireland in *Crindle Investments v. Wymes* ([1998] 4 I.R. 567).

Section 49 of the 1963 Act is effectively a statutory exception to this rule that the directors' duties are only owed to the company as a whole. It provides that where directors in a public company are re-

Company Law

sponsible for issuing a prospectus for investment which contains misleading information and which incurs "loss and damage which has been sustained by reason of an untrue statement contained therein", the directors will be liable to compensate the affected parties.

12.2.2 The creditors

From recent case law, it would appear that the duties that the directors owe to the company transfer to the creditors when a company becomes insolvent. The rationale of this is that the assets of the company are now being held on trust for the creditors, and the directors no longer have power to deal with them. In *Re Frederick Inns* ([1994] 1 I.L.R.M. 387), the directors of a group of companies which were insolvent, made payments to the Revenue on behalf of other companies in the group. The court held that these payments were *ultra vires* the capacity of the companies and also stated that the directors owed a general duty to creditors of the company once the company becomes insolvent. They must not do anything with the company assets that would diminish the funds which are now held beneficially for the creditors. In the case of *Nicholson v. Permakraft* ([1985] 1 N.Z.L.R. 242), the court referred to the duty existing to the creditors, even when the company is of doubtful solvency, *i.e.* the minds of the directors should be addressing their duties to the creditors.

12.2.3 The employees

Section 52 of the Companies Act 1990 imposed a duty on the directors to have regard to the interests of the employees of the company. It has been noted that this duty may, on occasion, be in conflict with the duty to act in the interests of the company as a whole, *e.g.* in relation to industrial disputes, etc. At common law it had not been felt that there was any duty owed by directors to the employees of the company, *Parke v. Daily News Ltd.* ([1961] 1 All E.R. 695).

12.3 The duties owed by directors

At common law the director has been deemed to have a number of duties:

   (i)   duty to act bona fide, for a proper purpose and for the benefit of the company;

   (ii) duty to use due care, skill and diligence in the exercise of their functions;

(iii) duty to disclose any personal interest or profit which may come in conflict with the interests of the company.

12.3.1   Duty to act bona fide, for a proper purpose and for the benefit of the company

This duty to act *bona fide*, for a proper purpose and for the benefit of the company, is deemed to be a subjective duty and, in the case of *Re Smith & Fawcett Ltd.* ([1942] 2 All E.R. 542), Lord Greene said that the directors "must exercise their discretion *bona fide* in what they consider, not what the court may consider, to be in the best interest of the company". Therefore, the onus of proof will lie on the plaintiff to show that there has been bad faith in the making of a particular decision before the court will make such a finding against the director. It must be noted that, whilst a director has acted beyond his powers and therefore in breach of his duty to the company, the particular act in question may be ratified by the company in general meeting. If this is not done, then an action can be taken against the director by the company, usually to recover losses, or by the shareholders in a section 205 application.

In the case of *Re Hafner* ([1920] I.R. 107), a transfer of shares to the plaintiff had not been approved by the directors. He claimed that this decision was activated by a desire to keep him out of the company as he would only challenge the exorbitant salaries that the directors were paying themselves. The directors refused to answer the allegation, and when the transferee was able to provide evidence that in fact there were, exorbitant salaries, the Supreme Court held that there was bad faith in relation to the making of the decision. In *Clark v. Workman* ([1959] A.C. 324), it was found that a director who had fettered his discretion in telling an outsider that he would vote in a particular way had acted in bad faith towards the company, and that the whole board was tainted by the fact, as his was the casting vote on a decision as to whether or not to transfer shares. In *G&S Doherty Ltd. v. Doherty* (unreported, High Court, December 1969), the court was satisfied that the particular allotment of the shares by the directors was an improper use of their fiduciary powers as its sole purpose was to remove the plaintiff from the company and was therefore not made in good faith.

In the case of *Howard Smith v. Ampol* ([1974] A.C. 821), the court held that, in deciding whether a power had been used for the proper purpose, one must look at the wording of the articles. In doing so, the court found in this case that there was an improper use of the power to allot new shares, as its purpose was to make someone a majority shareholder and that was an attack on the principle of majority rule within a company, *i.e.* that the directors could, by allotment, abolish the existing majority. Similarly in *Nash v. Lancegaye* ((1958) I.L.T.R. 11), the court set aside the issue of shares as it was simply an attempt to ensure continued control within the company. In all of these cases, the directors had been given the power to allot shares by the company in general meeting or by the articles (section 20 of the 1983 Act), but they cannot abuse that power and allot for improper purposes. If they are seen to do so, the allotment can be cast aside.

12.3.2 Duty to use due care, skill and diligence in the exercise of their functions

Directors are not required to have any particular qualification and nor must they have any particular skill. There is no proper benchmark as to what standard they should live up to. Nevertheless, this does not constitute a licence to be irresponsible, and a director may be liable according to the general principles set down by Romer J. in *Re City Equitable Fire Insurance Company* ([1925] Ch. 407): "a director need not show a greater degree of skill than may reasonably be expected from a person of his knowledge and experience."

This test is partially objective as it refers to the standard of the reasonable man, but it is mainly subjective as it is based on the knowledge, skill and experience of the particular director. Therefore, the level of skill required of the director will only be that which he possesses. In *Aberdeen Railway Co. v. Blaike Bros.* ([1854] Macq. 461), Lord Cranworth stated: "It was the director's duty to give his co-directors, and through them to the company, the full benefit of all the knowledge and skill which he could bring to bear on the subject". In *Dorchester Finance Co. Ltd. v. Stebbing* ([1989] B.C.L.C. 489), two non-executive directors were held jointly liable with the executive director for losses incurred by the latter, because the court felt that if they had used their professional accounting skills, the losses would have been averted.

12.3.2.1 A director cannot be held liable for errors of judgement

As a matter of commercial reality, directors must take business risks and that which may have seemed proper at the time cannot be struck down by the court with the benefit of hindsight. The director is entitled to make a judgement call. In *Re Brazilian Rubber Plantations* ([1911]

1 Ch. 437), Neville J. stated that they must take reasonable care, to be measured by the care an ordinary man might take in the circumstances on his own behalf. However, if a director puts himself forward as having a greater degree of skill and experience than he actually possesses, and the company relies on this, then the director will be expected to exercise that higher standard of skill, *Chaudhry v. Prabhakar* ([1988] All E.R. 718). It would appear from the case of *Re Mont Clare Hotels Ltd.; Jackson v. Mortell*, (unreported, December 2, 1968), that to be found guilty of breach of duty, something more than mere carelessness is required.

12.3.2.2 A director is not required to give continuous attention to the affairs of the company, but to give reasonable attention
The level of attention will obviously depend on the type of director, the position and the salary. A managing director will have a higher requirement placed on him as regards the attendance to company affairs. A director will not be in breach of duty just because he fails to attend all of the board meetings, *Perry's Case* ((1876) 34 L.T. 716), and also the failure of a director to attend the meetings cannot make him liable for irregular actions which were taken in a meeting from which he was absent, *Marquis of Bute's Case* ([1892] 2 Ch. 100). However, the court may interpret different levels of duties owed by directors in different cases. In *Jackson v. Munster Bank Ltd.* ((1885) 15 L.R. Ir. 356), the company had joint operations in Cork and Dublin and whilst the director had gone to all of the Dublin meetings, he had attended few in Cork. He was found liable for the losses which were incurred due to the fact that the directors at the Cork meetings had made loans to themselves which were irrecoverable. He was found liable for the losses, because evidence was produced that he had been notified of irregularities, but had failed to investigate same.

12.3.2.3 A director may delegate duties to persons who, having regard to the organisation of the business, are proper persons to exercise those functions
In any company, it is essential that the director can delegate functions to other persons as set out in the articles. In the case of *Dovey v. Corry* ([1901] Ch. 477), it was held that a director could not have eyes everywhere and turn himself into an auditor, managing director and chairman. The case centred around the reliance by the directors on a particular set of figures in the balance sheet which set out a profit, yet the sheet had been fraudulently prepared. The House of Lords held that the director was not in breach of duty and said that a business could

not function if people could not trust those who are put into a position of trust for the express purpose of attending to details of management. However, it has been noted that the director could be in breach of duty if there were grounds for suspecting the incompetence or fraudulent intent of the official.

Generally, it is felt that the standard of care, skill and diligence required is quite low, which therefore results in very little litigation against directors relating to managerial incompetence. As the law stands, the company is really the only credible plaintiff in a case against directors for negligence. As the directors are the controllers of the company, action will *usually* only be taken where a company is being wound up and the liquidator instigates proceedings.

12.3.3 *Duty to disclose any personal interest or profit which may come in conflict with the interests of the company*

The rationale behind this duty is that the director cannot be allowed to receive benefit and profit as a result of his position as director. The law would deem that the director holds such profits on trust for the company as a whole. The case of *Regal (Hastings) v. Gulliver* ([1942] 1 All E.R. 378) is authority for the strict ruling that a director must account for all such profits which he makes as a result of his position, even though there has been nothing improper in what has been done nor has the company suffered a loss. In that case, the directors of a company bought up shares in a subsidiary so that the subsidiary might have the required amount of capital to acquire the lease of cinemas. When the lease of the cinemas was acquired, the directors then sold the shares in the company and the subsidiary and made a profit in doing so, as they had shares in the subsidiary. The new owners (shareholders in company) then claimed that this profit was now due to be paid back into the company. The House of Lords agreed, stating that even though the directors were compelled to buy the shares to raise the capital of the subsidiary, and had therefore done nothing wrong, they still had a duty to account for the profits to the company, *i.e.* they had only acquired the benefit through their position and knowledge as directors. The same rationale was used in the case of *Industrial Development v. Cooley* ([1972] 2 All E.R. 162) in that a director must not divert to himself personally a business opportunity which the company would otherwise have, because the director is a fiduciary and is abusing his position, as it is only through his position that he could acquire the relevant information.

In the *Cooley* case the managing director of a construction company whose proposals for a particular project were rejected by the prospective customer, took sick leave from work and took on the contract in a personal capacity. It was found that he was in a position to seek out this contract because of his position within the company and that he could not therefore benefit from profits received, but was to hold them on trust for the company.

12.4 Contracts involving the directors and the company

Prima facie, this duty to avoid conflicts of interest with the company will also arise if the director enters into a contract with the company or if the director has an interest in another company or firm which is to contract with the company. It has been stated that these transactions are voidable at the instance of the company but it is also equally possible for the company to ratify such a transaction in the general meeting. Usually, the company articles will include an Article 85-type provision that will expressly allow for such transactions to be entered into by the directors. However, section 194 of the Companies Act 1963 which is amended by sections 27 and 47 of the 1990 Act now provides that, for such transactions to be valid, the directors must first have made full disclosure of their interest, whether direct or indirect, to the board of directors. This disclosure is essential and will surely be a pre-condition to the reliance on the Article 85-type provision, and indeed companies may well write this duty to disclose into the article. In *Guinness plc v. Saunders* ([1988] 2 All E.R. 940), it was stated that the disclosure must be to the full board and not just to a subsection. Failure to disclose will render the contract voidable, *i.e.* the general meeting could still agree to sanction it, but if it is declared void, the director must account to the company for any profits made thereunder.

12.5 Statutory duties of the director

The above duty referred to in section 194 of the Companies Act 1963 and amended by sections 27 and 47 of the Companies Act 1990 imposes a statutory duty of disclosure on the directors. Other statutory provisions also impose duties on the directors. Section 53 of the Companies Act 1990 requires the director to notify the company of his interest in the company shares and the amount in which he has an interest.

Company Law

Section 202 of the 1990 Act imposes a duty on the directors to keep proper books of account and section 203 imposes penalties on the directors for failing to do so. Section 204 imposes personal liability on the directors for the losses of the company if it is deemed that the losses were caused by the failure to keep proper books of account. The legislation seeks to create a tighter set of rules and regulations to govern the actions of directors. We will examine the actions which can be taken against directors in misfeasance, reckless trading, fraudulent trading and insider trading in chapter 20. Aside from these statutory actions, the usual forms of action against the errant director will be taken by the company. If he is guilty of negligence against the company which has incurred damage, then he will be liable to the company for the losses. Where the director has breached duty and trust or has derived benefit from the company, the company can take a common law action against him for account of the profits or losses or could seek equitable relief in the form of an injunction or declaration.

13. THE COMPANY ACCOUNTS

13.1   The books of account

Section 202 of the Companies Act 1990 requires companies to keep and maintain proper books of account on a continuous and consistent basis and replaces the somewhat limited requirements of section 147 of the 1963 Act. Books of account in any company must set out the assets and liabilities of the company, the nature and extent of expenditure, the level of sales or services, including all invoices for same and a note of all stock within the company. The accounts must give a "true and fair view of the state of affairs of the company" and must be kept at the registered office of the company and be made available for inspection by the directors and their accountants at reasonable times. Section 203 of the Act permits the court to impose penalties on the officers of the company which is being wound up and which has been unable to pay its debts, where proper books of account have not been kept. Section 204 then permits the court to impose personal liability on an officer of the company where the company has been wound up and where the court is of the belief that the failure to keep proper books of account contributed to the failure of the company.

13.2   Size of companies

For the purposes of the keeping of books of account, the preparing of annual accounts and the making of annual returns to the Registrar, the Companies Act 1986 distinguishes small, medium and large-sized companies and imposes less strict requirements in relation to the accounts on the smaller companies. Under section 8, a company is small if its balance sheet total does not exceed £1,500,000, its turnover does not exceed £3,000,000 and the average number of persons employed within the company does not exceed 50. Section 11 provides that a medium company is one whose balance sheet does not exceed £6,000,000, its turnover does not exceed £12,000,000 and the average number of persons employed within the company does not exceed 250. All other companies are deemed to be large. The different rules relating to the accounting requirements of each company are referred to below.

Company Law

13.3   The annual accounts

Under section 148 of the Companies Act 1963, the directors are required to prepare a balance sheet and profit and loss account which they must put before the members of the company at the annual general meeting. They must also furnish a directors' report and an auditors' report to the meeting which verify and explain the balance sheet and accounts. Again, the aim of the accounts is to give a true and fair view of the state of affairs at the end of the financial year, taking into account all profits and losses made and to put all necessary information before the members for inspection. There is a requirement to comply with accepted accountancy standards when completing accounts within the company and section 5 of the 1986 Act sets out certain accounting principles which are to be applied in the completion of accounts. On foot of the European Communities (Companies) (Group Accounts) Regulations 1992, it is now a requirement that holding companies keep consolidated accounts showing the state of affairs of the entire group of companies, including all of the subsidiaries. Obviously, the level of involvement of one company with another will decide whether they are a "group" of companies for the purposes of this requirement.

13.3.1   The balance sheet

This sets out the assets of the company and how they are distinguished as capital and reserves. The balance sheet sets out the level of investment in the company and how that investment has been utilised in the acquisition of assets etc. The balance sheet should set out the share capital and debentures of the company, fixed assets, reserves of capital, information on debts owed and details of guarantees given. The balance sheet will not give an exact guide to the value of the company because the assets listed may have diminished or increased in value and the accounting method must take this into account. The Companies Act 1986 requires directors to maintain the same format from year to year in the preparation of the balance sheet. A "small company" need only draw up an abridged balance sheet for presentation at the annual general meeting which would show an aggregate value of the assets. All other companies must set out detailed breakdowns.

13.3.2   The profit and loss account

As its title suggests, this is a detailed description of the profits and losses made by the company in the year prior to the annual general meeting and aims to inform the members of the true state of affairs within the company. There are various formats which the account can take and it must include various breakdowns on turnover and operating costs to be included. Small and medium-sized companies are exempted from some of the more detailed requirements regarding the completing of the profit and loss account.

13.3.3   *Miscellaneous requirements*

A *directors' report* must be put before the annual general meeting and must comment on the state of the company's business, refer to the paying out of dividends or the placing of profits in reserves. Failure to comply with the requirements relating to the report will result in fines or imprisonment for a director, section 15 of the Companies (Amendment) Act 1982. Sections 41 and 42 of the Companies Act 1990 require that all exempted transactions whereby directors have secured loans, quasi-loans and guarantees from the company must be included in a statement accompanying the accounts and section 191 of the Companies Act 1963 requires that all particulars of directors' salaries must be included with the accounts in order that the members can inspect same. The directors are also required to put an *auditors' report* before the annual general meeting and this is discussed below.

13.4   The auditors

Since the enactment of the Companies Act 1963, all companies are required to have their accounts examined every year by an independent, professionally qualified auditor who will prepare a report thereon. Section 160 of the Companies Act 1963 provides that every company shall appoint auditors at the annual general meeting and that they shall remain in office for the year. It is possible for the company to remove auditors by ordinary resolution, but an extended notice period must be given to the auditor and he has a right to be heard in the meeting.

The auditor is deemed to be an officer of the company and acts as an agent of the company when he is carrying out his duties under the Acts. Section 187 of the Companies Act 1990 requires the auditor to be a qualified accountant and section 163 of the Companies Act 1963 states that the auditor must make out a report to the members on the accounts which he has examined, and must also make out a report on all of the balance sheets and profit and loss accounts which are put before the general meeting. The auditors must set out whether they have received all relevant information and whether in their opinion, proper books of account have been kept and whether, in their opinion, the accounts give the information which is required by the Acts. Under section 15 of the Companies Act 1986 the auditors are required to consider whether the information given by the directors in their report is consistent with the accounts for the year. In *Re Kingston Cotton Mill Co. (No.2)* ([1896] 2 Ch. 279), Lord Lopes said that the law treats the auditor as a "watchdog, not a bloodhound". In *Thomas Gerrard & Sons Ltd.* ([1968] Ch. 455), the auditors were held liable where a managing director had falsified the accounts by altering certain invoices. It was felt that the auditors had breached their duty to the company by failing to examine these alterations and make further checks on foot of them. The standard applied to the auditor is of the careful and competent auditor who will exercise reasonable skill. If the company suffers loss as a result of the negligence of the auditor, then he will be liable to the company. It is also clear that the auditor may be liable to other persons who relied on the reports and perhaps made investments in the company on foot of the reports. In *Caparo Industries plc v. Dickman* ([1990] B.C.L.C. 273), the House of Lords said that the auditor did not owe a duty to the world at large or to potential investors but rather to those parties with whom he had established a relationship, *i.e.* that there was reliance by the other party on the information provided by the auditor and that the auditor was aware of this reliance. The court said that the carrying-out of an audit was part of a scheme which was designed to protect the company itself and to make information available to those persons who had an interest in the financial stability of the company.

13.5   Annual returns

As well as maintaining the books of account and placing the balance sheet and profit and loss account before the members in the annual general meeting, the company is also required by sections 125–129 of the Companies Act 1963 to make an annual return to the Registrar of Companies. The return will include details of the company capital and the shares and investments of members and directors, the indebtedness of the company, details on further allotment of shares and all other relevant matters. Until the 1986 Act, it was not necessary for companies to attach their balance sheet and profit and loss account to the annual return but this is now required by that Act and the accounts must be verified by the directors. The reports of the auditors must also be included. However, exemptions are created here, depending on the size of the company. Section 10(1) of that Act exempts "small" companies from furnishing the profit and loss account and directors' report with their return, and it is also permitted to file an *abridged* balance sheet. The medium-sized company must file all of the documents but is permitted to furnish an *abridged* balance sheet with the annual return and a less detailed profit and loss account. It must be noted, however, that despite the relaxed requirements on small and medium-sized companies, they still have the duty to provide a "true and fair account of the state of affairs of the company". The company is required to make the annual return to the Registrar within 60 days of the annual general meeting and failure to do so can result in a fine. If a company has failed to make a return for a year or more, the Registrar had the power under section 12 of the 1982 Act to strike that company off the register for such failure. This provision has now been replaced by section 46 of the Companies (Amendment) (No. 2) Act 1999 which also enables the Registrar to strike a company off the register on receipt of notification from the Revenue Commissioners that the company has failed to deliver a statement which is required by the Taxes Consolidation Act 1997. Under section 311 of the Companies Act 1963 (as inserted by section 246 of the 1990 Act), the Registrar can restore the company to the register within 12 months of the strike-off, if the application is made by the company and the necessary returns have been filed. After the lapse of 12 months, the application must be made to the court seeking restoration of the company to the register. This court application has been extended by section 46 of the Companies (Amendment) (No. 2) Act 1999 and provides that such an application can now be made in the Circuit Court.

14. THE RAISING AND MAINTENANCE OF CAPITAL

14.1 Introduction

A company can raise the necessary capital to finance itself in a number of ways. It can issue shares to its members and thereby obtain investment share capital, it can borrow capital from lending institutions, it can perhaps acquire grants from the State to start up business, and, if the company is profitable, it can expand the business through acquired profits. However, when we refer to the *capital of the company* it is generally the *share capital* which is referred to, *i.e.* the capital which is raised upon the investment of the shareholders. In Chapter 8, we examined the manner in which shares are issued and the different types of shares which can be issued.

14.2 Types of share capital

14.2.1 The authorised share capital

This is the amount of capital as stated in the memorandum of association and it represents the limit or extent of capital which the company is authorised to issue. This will generally be set as a high figure and in most companies only a fraction of that amount is actually issued to shareholders. The *authorised share capital* can be increased by the members through an alteration of the clause in the memorandum. This alteration must be permitted by the articles and if Article 44 of the model articles were applied, the alteration could be effected by ordinary resolution.

14.2.2 The issued share capital

This is the total value of the shares which have actually been issued to shareholders for money or money's worth. The individual shares will have a nominal or par value, *e.g.* £1 or £5 per share and may be fully or partly paid up by the member. In a public limited company, 25 per cent of the value of the share must be paid up at the time of issue. The *issued share capital* can therefore be divided into the *paid up share capital* and the *uncalled capital* which the members have agreed to pay up when a *call* is made. Obviously, the actual value of the shares will fluctuate depending on the success of the company and the issued share capital cannot exceed the *authorised share capital*.

14.2.3 The reserve capital

A company may pass a special resolution that a certain amount of its uncalled share capital shall not be called up, except in the event of the company being wound up and is therefore in reserve for that purpose.

14.2.4   *Miscellaneous share capital*

Where shares are issued at a premium, *i.e.* where the shareholder pays a sum in excess of the nominal or par value of the share, the amount of the excess or premium paid, is lodged into an account known as the *share premium account.* This sum has to be dealt with as capital, because it is not a profit. The proceeds of the share premium account can be used to issue bonus shares to shareholders at a later date. Since Part XI of the 1990 Act was enacted, a company has been permitted to issue *redeemable shares, i.e.* the share can be redeemed by the shareholder and the company will pay back the investment at a set time. However, when this repayment is made from profits or through the proceeds of a fresh issue, the share could be cancelled and thus reduce the nominal value of the issued share capital. Therefore, an amount equivalent to that which was paid back to the shareholder must be transferred to what is known as the *capital redemption reserve fund* which will ensure that the original capital structure remains intact.

14.3   The maintenance of capital

The law has always recognised the importance of maintaining the issued share capital which is invested within the company, essentially to protect creditors of the company who have loaned money to the company on the strength of this capital. However, this protection of creditors is notional, as some companies today may have an issued share capital of £5 and in many cases creditors would not check the level of issued share capital.

In the past, there was a complete prohibition on the reduction of capital by a company, except where the reduction simply occurred by virtue of failed business. There was also a total restriction on the returning of investment to the shareholder as this was viewed as a returning of capital to the member. There was also a rule that companies could not purchase their own shares or indirectly finance the purchase of their own shares, as this could enable a company to acquire control over its own capital to the detriment of shareholders and creditors and thereby capital would be affected. All of these rules have been relaxed by legislation, but with very specific conditions to be met in each case.

14.4   The redemption of shares

As explained above, the issue of redeemable shares was at first prohibited, and was only relaxed in the Companies Act 1963 to provide
for the issue of *redeemable preference shares*. Now, since the introduction
of section 207 of the 1990 Act, a company is permitted to issue *ordinary redeemable shares* providing that at least 10 per cent of the company's shareholding is not redeemable. These issues are permitted because the law has required the company to either pay the redeemable
sum from profits or from the fresh issue of shares and then to either
cancel the shares or retain them as treasury shares, which are effectively "frozen" shares with no rights attaching, which can be re-issued
at a value set by section 209(6) of the 1990 Act. The transfer of the
equivalent sum which was paid out, into the capital redemption reserve fund ensures that whilst the nominal value of the issued share
capital is reduced, a sum equal in value is lodged in the fund, and the
capital, whilst altered, is replaced elsewhere. Therefore, the procedure
does not breach the rules of capital maintenance.

14.5   The company acquiring its own shares

In the case of *Trevor v. Whitworth* ([1887] 12 A.C. 409), the House of
Lords set out the basic rule that a company could not directly acquire
its own shares. It was felt that if a company could acquire its own
shares, the rights of shareholders and creditors would be affected, as
the company could then control its own capital, *i.e.* the company could
invest in itself, with whatever funds were available. It was also felt that
directors of the company could control the price of the shares which
would be detrimental to the other company shareholders. Most im-
portantly, it was felt that if a company was permitted to purchase its
own shares, it was likely that they would be purchased with capital,
and this was contrary to the rules on capital maintenance. This restriction was set out in section 72 of the Companies Act 1963 and added
to by section 41 of the 1983 Act which provided four exceptions to
the general restriction whereby the company *could* acquire its own
shares:

(i)   where the shares were acquired otherwise than for valuable consideration, *e.g.* where the company was acting
as an executor;

(ii)   where the shares were redeemed, *i.e.* the company buying the shares back;

(iii) where the company were ordered to buy the shares by an order of the court, *e.g.* on foot of a section 205 application, the court orders the company to buy out the shareholder;

(iv) where the shares have been forfeited or surrendered, *i.e.* the company is effectively acquiring the shares back.

However, as in other jurisdictions, the restriction was further relaxed through the Companies Act 1990 which took on board the Second E.U. Directive which provided that such a transaction should be permitted, provided that certain pre-conditions were met and therefore greatly adds to the exceptions listed above.

The 1990 Act distinguishes between *market* and *off-market purchases* of shares. The *market purchase* would involve a company buying its own shares on a recognised stock exchange, and will therefore apply to public companies. Section 215 of the 1990 Act requires that, in order to carry out this purchase, the company must be authorised by the company in general meeting, yet this authority can be a general authority lasting for a specific period of time and specifying the maximum number of shares which can be purchased and the maximum and minimum amount payable for the shares. The *off-market purchase* of shares will involve a private company purchasing its own shares in a private contract. Under section 213 of the 1990 Act, this specific contract must be authorised by a special resolution of the company. A copy of the contract must be furnished to the members at least 21 days in advance of the meeting or be furnished at the meeting. The company can only purchase these shares if they have already been fully paid up, and the purchase can only be out of distributable profits or the proceeds of a new issue. The shares may be cancelled when purchased or retained as treasury shares and an amount equivalent to that paid for the shares must be transferred to the capital redemption reserve fund, in order to ensure that there is no effect on capital structure. A company which has purchased its own shares must send details of same to the Registrar of Companies and keep all such contracts in the registered office for perusal by members. Failure to do this would result in a fine.

Section 219 of the Companies Act 1990 provides that a company cannot be sued for specific performance if it is unable to meet the contract for redemption or purchase of shares if it can show that it does not have the distributable profits available. Section 42 of the

1983 Act prevents a company circumventing the original restriction on purchasing their own shares by having a nominee purchase the shares.

14.6 The company providing financial assistance for the purchase of its own shares

Section 60 of the Companies Act 1963 prohibits the company giving financial assistance for the purchase of its own shares, as this was looked upon as having the same potential effect on capital as the direct purchase of its own shares by the company. The 1990 Act made no changes in this section. However, section 60 set out five specific exceptions to the rule and also included the proviso in relation to private companies that the transaction *could* be authorised if the company had passed a special resolution in the 12 months prior to the purchase specifically sanctioning the purchase, and if other essential conditions were met. This proviso did not apply to public companies.

The five *specific* exceptions which are set out in section 60 permit the company to provide financial assistance for the purchase of its shares and they are:

(i)   where the company pays out a dividend properly declared by the company, *i.e.* facilitating further investment from the shareholder;

(ii) where the company has to pay out a liability which was lawfully incurred, *e.g.* indirect payment towards purchase of shares;

(iii) where the company lends money in the course of its business, *i.e.* lending is the company business;

(iv) where the company has an employee share scheme in place, which provides assistance to employees or former employees, including directors with salaried office, for the purchase of shares in the company;

(v)   where the company makes loans to persons other than directors, who are *bona fide* in the employment of the company to permit them acquire shares in the company.

Other than these specific exceptions, section 60 then set out the proviso that a special resolution could be passed by the company sanctioning the giving of assistance in a particular transaction and that it had to be accompanied by a declaration from the directors setting out all of the details regarding the proposed transaction and the parties involved. Failure to comply with these requirements would render the transaction invalid, as the prohibition would then apply (unless it was within the five exceptions).

In *Re Northside Motor Co. Ltd. Eddison v. Allied Irish Banks Ltd.* (unreported, High Court, July 24, 1985) Costello J. found a transaction to be in breach of section 60. In this case, a company had guaranteed a loan from a bank to a subsidiary company. The loan had been incurred by the subsidiary to enable it buy shares in the company. However, the company was called upon to pay on foot of the guarantee and this was considered to bring the transaction within section 60, *i.e.* the company was indirectly financing the purchase of its shares. However, a special resolution had not been passed authorising the transaction and the necessary declarations were not put forward, therefore the transaction was invalid, *i.e.* it could not avail of the proviso. In the case of *Lombard & Ulster Banking Limited v. Bank of Ireland* (unreported, High Court, June 2, 1987), Costello J. stated that the party seeking to uphold the transaction had to show that the requisite resolutions and declarations had been furnished and that the transaction had been properly validated within the company. However, in that case the court felt that the bank was not on notice of any invalidity and upheld the transaction.

14.7 Reduction of capital

Capital can be lost in the ordinary course of business and the law acknowledges that this is the case. However, section 40 of the 1983 Act provides that where the capital falls below a defined level, *i.e.* where the net assets are half or less of the amount of the company's called-up share capital, the directors must convene an extraordinary general meeting. This provision acts as a safeguard to shareholders where there has been a serious decrease in capital and to draw their attention to the matter. If the directors fail to call such a meeting, they are open to fines or imprisonment.

Other than this natural reduction in capital, a company is not permitted to reduce its share capital other than by permission of the court. This is again an attempt to ensure that the company's capital remains intact. A company could seek to reduce its share capital if it has more capital than it requires or is paying high interest on the excess. If this is the case, the court could sanction that the excess be paid back to the shareholders or their liability extinguished in relation to it. Under section 72(2) of the 1963 Act, the company can then pass a special resolution to this effect. At this court hearing, the company creditors can be heard as the reduction may affect them.

A company could also seek to reduce its share capital because it has lost a significant part of its capital due to trading losses and depreciation of assets. The application to have the capital reduced will really only mean an amendment to the balance sheet to bring the capital into line with the assets and to write off the debit balance, thereby enabling the company to declare a dividend on profits. The decision to reduce capital must be made fairly and equitably and once the court has sanctioned this, the special resolution must be passed ensuring that 75 per cent of the company are behind this move.

14.8   Dividends and distributions

As noted in Chapter 8, an individual member has a right to have a dividend paid out when one is declared by the general meeting, upon the recommendations of the directors. Section 45(1) of the 1983 Act sets out one of the fundamental rules of capital maintenance in that distributions or dividends may only be paid out of *profits* and not out of the capital of the company. Section 51 of that Act, however, excludes certain disposals of assets from the definition of *"distribution"*. Therefore, a distribution can be made to members, from sources *other than profits* where it involves: an issue of fully or partly paid up bonus shares; the redemption or purchase of shares; a reduction of the share capital authorised by section 72 of the 1963 Act; or a distribution of the assets of a company upon the winding up of that company. All of the above are referred to in the preceding paragraphs.

Section 45(2) of the 1983 Act defines the company's profits available for distribution (*i.e.* for its dividends) as:

> "its accumulated, realised profits, so far as not previously utilised by distribution or capitalisation, less its accumulated, realised losses, so far as not previously written off in a reduction or reorganisation of capital duly made."

The realised profits available include any surplus made on the profit and loss account in a given year. *Accumulated* refers to any surplus from previous years which has not been distributed but has been placed in the reserves. A capital surplus made on the revaluation of a fixed asset does not constitute a realised profit and is therefore not available for distribution to the members, section 149(6) of the Companies Act 1963. However, any surplus made upon the actual sale of an asset is realised and is therefore available for distribution.

The company must deduct its *accumulated realised losses* in order to determine the sum available for distribution. Losses which have been written off by a reduction in capital or some other re-organisation of capital do not have to be deducted. The amount will include current losses and the losses from previous years.

A public limited company is prohibited from making a distribution unless its net assets are equal to, or exceed the sum of, its called-up share capital and *undistributable reserves*, and the distribution does not reduce the amount of those assets to less than that sum. The *undistributable reserves* are: the share premium account; the capital redemption reserve fund; the excess of its accumulated unrealised profits over its accumulated unrealised losses; and any other reserve which the company is prohibited from distributing, whether by enactment or memorandum.

In circumstances where a dividend is paid out of capital, the directors may be held liable for breach of duty. However, under section 50 of the 1983 Act, where the member in receipt of the dividend was aware or ought reasonably have known that the distribution came out of the company's capital, or was otherwise unlawful, then the member is bound to repay the sum.

15. BORROWING – DEBENTURES AND CHARGES

15.1 Introduction

A company will generally be authorised to borrow money in its memorandum of association. If this authority is not expressly stated, it will be readily implied if the borrowing can be deemed to be incidental to the objects of the company. For many private companies, which have minimal investment capital, borrowing from banks and lending institutions is the main way in which the company obtains the finance it needs to carry on its business. Under section 6 of the Companies (Amendment) Act 1983, a public limited company cannot exercise its borrowing powers until it secures the necessary certificate from the Registrar.

The company may borrow money from investors who will then have debentures in the company evidencing that loan. In some cases, debenture holders will not have required security for their investments and will be recognised as unsecured creditors. However, in order to secure advances of capital from the banks or lending institutions, the company must generally give some form of security for the loan and this power to give security will be incidental to the power to borrow. The company can create a legal or an equitable mortgage over its real or leasehold property in favour of the lender, or it can create a fixed or floating charge over its assets in favour of the lender. The means of providing security and the various forms of security available will be examined below.

15.2 Debentures

A debenture is the instrument or document by which a company acknowledges the debt which it owes to its creditor. Debentures can be one of a series, they can require payment of interest on the debt, they can require repayment of the principal sum on a specified date or occurrence, and in many cases they contain a charge on the company's property securing the debt, and thereby constitute a *secured debenture*.

A debenture holder is therefore someone who has advanced capital to the company, but unlike the shareholder who has invested, the debenture holder does not become a member of the company. The debenture holder is entitled to be paid a fixed rate of interest on his advance, regardless of whether the company has made profits or not.

The company can issue a series of debentures to different creditors on identical terms, but it is also common to issue *debenture stock*. This involves the company obtaining advances from a number of different sources and placing all sums into a single loan fund, whereupon the individual lenders can then be issued with stock certificates setting out the percentage of the fund which belongs to them. The debenture holder can then sell or transfer part of his investment or advance to others as it is a valuable asset. Section 81 of the Companies Act 1963 would require that the transfer be registered with the Registrar, except where a bearer debenture is being transferred. The debenture stock is constituted by a *trust deed* which provides for the security and provides that a trustee is appointed by the company to act on behalf of the stockholders.

Where the advance has been secured by a charge, the debenture will set out the nature of the charge which has been created as security for the debt, the assets, property or undertaking over which the charge exists and the remedies available to the debenture holder if the company default on repayments of the loan. The debenture holder will thus have a direct interest in the company's assets over which his charge exists.

15.3   Charges

In the context of the debtor/creditor relationship in company law, a *charge* involves the transfer of some *proprietary interest* in the company assets to the lending institution in order to secure the repayment of the advance by the company. In *Re Clare Textiles* (unreported, High Court, February 1, 1993), Costello J. said that the charge is based on a contract, "under the terms of which certain property is available as security to meet the performance of a liability, usually the payment of money". The chargee (lending institution) acquires certain rights in respect of the charged assets which can be pursued in the event of the company defaulting on repayment. These remedies will involve obtaining an order for sale of the assets or appointing a receiver to deal with the assets. Legal and equitable *mortgages* of land are different from company charges in that there is full transfer of title in the land to the lender until such time as the advance is repaid. As stated above, the creation of the charge simply gives the chargeholder a proprietary interest in the assets from the time the charge is created. There are two main types of company charges, the *fixed charge* and the *floating charge*.

15.4 Fixed charges

A fixed charge is one which is created in favour of a lender and which is created over a *specific identifiable item of property*, *e.g.* land, buildings or plant and machinery. The specific assets over which the charge is created should be clearly set out in the debenture and will therefore permit the chargeholder to appoint a receiver to sell or dispose of those particular assets if there is default on the repayment of the loan. A fixed charge must be registered pursuant to section 99 of the Companies Act 1963 in order to secure its position. However, fixed charges are inappropriate for fluctuating assets, *e.g.* the stock-in-trade or raw materials which may make up a large part of the company's assets and could be offered as security. Therefore, *floating charges* were created.

15.5 Floating charges

A floating charge is a charge which can be created over a class or classes of assets, the contents of which are constantly changing. The floating charge does not attach to any specific asset at the time of its creation, but is seen to hover over the entire class of assets over which it was created, which in many cases can consist of "all of the assets and undertaking of the company". A company could therefore secure a loan by creating a floating charge, in favour of the lender, over the company's stock-in-trade, its raw materials or over the debts owed to the company itself. These assets will be changing on a day-to-day basis, as the company is free to deal with the assets in the ordinary course of their business. Assets may be withdrawn by sale and proceeds take their place, other assets may be substituted or additional assets added by trading, but floating security follows the concern, which is reduced or added to through all stages of trading. The great benefit of a floating charge for the company is that they have been able to secure finance from a lending institution by virtue of what appears on their balance sheet, but they are still free to continue to use and dispose of the charged property. In *Illingsworth v. Houldsworth* ([1904] A.C. 355), the court said that:

> "... a floating charge on the other hand is ambulatory and shifting in nature, hovering over and so to speak floating with the property which it intended to affect until some event occurs or some act is done which causes it to settle and fasten on the subject of the charge within its reach and grasp".

The acts referred to which cause a floating charge to crystallise are the appointing of a receiver, the winding up of the company or where the company ceases to do business as a going concern.

In the case of *Re Yorkshire Woolcombers Case* ([1903] 2 Ch. 284) Romer L.J. said that a floating charge would have the following characteristics:

(i)   if it is a charge on a class of assets of a company present and future;

(ii) if that class is one which in the ordinary course of business would be changing from time to time; and

(iii) if you find that by the charge it is contemplated that, until some future step is taken by or on behalf of those interested in the charge, the company may carry on its business in the ordinary way, so far as concerns the particular class of assets.

However, Romer L.J. pointed out that a charge could still be a floating charge without having all of these characteristics. In *Welch v. Bowmaker (Ireland) Limited and Bank of Ireland* ([1980] I.R. 251), the court found as a matter of construction, that the charge which had been created over a piece of company property was a floating charge, even though land was not an asset which would change from time to time.

15.6   Advantages of fixed charges over floating charges

It must be noted that a lending institution will prefer a fixed charge in terms of security and also because fixed charges cannot be affected by the legislative provisions which apply to floating charges upon winding up. First, if the company is wound up, the fixed chargeholder has priority over floating chargeholders whose charges have crystallised, perhaps over the same class of property, and can proceed to realise his secured asset. Under section 285 of the Companies Act 1963, floating charges also rank below the debts owed to the Revenue and to employees in the event of a winding up, and section 285(7)(b) provides that if there are insufficient assets to satisfy the preferential creditors, then the assets which are subject to floating charges can be used for this purpose. Section 288 of the Companies Act 1963, as amended by section 136 of the 1990 Act, provides that floating charges which are created within 12 months of a company being wound up are invalid unless it can be proven that the company was solvent at the time the

charge was created. The section allows the charge to remain valid for
the amount of cash that was forwarded to the company *at the time* of
creation of the charge. This is because the section aims to invalidate
charges which are created as securities at this time for cash advanced
in the past.

Section 136 of the 1990 Act provides that floating charges which
are created in favour of directors or "connected persons" within two
years of the winding up can be set aside. Also, under section 98 of the
Companies Act 1963, if a receiver is appointed on foot of a floating
charge and goes in to realise the assets, he must pay off the Revenue
as a preferential creditor out of the sums received, before he can pay
over sums to the holder of the charge. Where a receiver is appointed
under a floating charge over property which is *already* the subject of a
fixed charge, the receiver must yield priority to the fixed charge and
will be unable to do anything with the property without the consent
of the fixed chargeholder. It is also noted that lenders would prefer to
have security over a particular asset because the assets over which a
floating charge can be created, *e.g.* the assets as listed on the balance
sheets may actually be the subject of *retention of title* clauses. In that
case, the company does not own the asset, and the creditor may have
accepted a floating charge security believing that there were more assets within the particular class than was actually the case. Therefore,
the floating charge is open to much more legislative intervention than
the fixed charge.

15.7   Charges over book debts

A book debt is a debt which is owed to the company, concerned with
and arising from the company trade or business, which is entered or
commonly would be entered in the ordinary course of things in well
kept books of such a business or trade. Therefore, money owed to
the company is an asset that could be offered as security to a lender in
order to secure a loan. Because of the changing nature of the debts, it
was always accepted that a floating charge could be created over them.
However, banks and lending institutions were interested in securing
fixed charges over this form of security in order to avoid the restrictions placed upon floating charges upon winding up, etc. Charges were
therefore drawn up which provided that whilst the borrower company could still collect the book debts, he must transfer them to a
special account to which he would not have any further access, and

that this would essentially restrict the company from dealing with the assets and was therefore a fixed charge. In the cases of *Siebe Gorman v. Barclays Bank Ltd.* ([1977] 2 Lloyds Rep. 142) and *Re Keenan Brothers Ltd.* ([1985] I.R. 401), the courts held that the particular clauses at issue constituted fixed charges because they required the debts to be paid into a special bank account. In *Re A.H. Masser Ltd* ([1986] I.R. 445), Barron J. held the clause to constitute a fixed charge even though withdrawals from the account were not specifically prohibited. In *Re Wogan's (Drogheda) Ltd.* ([1993] 1 I.R. 157), the clause was held to constitute a fixed charge because it provided for a special bank account to be set up into which the debts would be transferred, despite the fact that no account had been specified after the debenture was created. In *Re Holidair Ltd.* ([1994] 1 I.R. 434), the Supreme Court reversed the High Court decision and held that the particular clause constituted a floating charge because, whilst the company was required to place the proceeds into a specific bank account, it was not restricted from withdrawing from the account and that therefore allowed the company to deal with the proceeds in the ordinary course of business. In that case it was noted that even if the parties have described the charge as a fixed charge, it is open to the court to decide what exactly the charge constitutes. The description of the charge is irrelevant. Therefore, given the present law, any bank or lending institution that seeks to have their charge over the book debts declared to be a fixed charge should ensure that all forms of restrictions are placed on the company as regards the special accounts and the company's access to such accounts. It is noted, however, that since the enactment of section 115 of the Finance Act 1996, a fixed charge over book debts ranks below the debts which are owed to the Revenue in the event of winding up. This does take away certain of the benefits which attached to a fixed charge over book debts.

15.8 The effect of floating charges

The flexibility of the floating charge has always been a cause of concern to creditors who have feared that their floating charge security could lose priority to a fixed charge which was created after the floating charge. A later fixed charge would gain priority over a previous floating charge as it specifies a particular asset from the time of creation. Also, a later floating charge can be created over a particular part of the assets covered by a previous floating charge over the wider

category of assets as held in *Re Automatic Bottle Makers* ([1926] 1 Ch.
412). Therefore, it is standard practice to insert a condition preventing the company from creating any subsequent charge which ranks in
priority or *pari passu* with the floating charge. This is known as a *negative pledge clause*. This prohibition will prevent greater or equal charges
being created over the same class of assets, provided that the subsequent chargee was *aware* of the restriction in the previous charge. It
has been set out in many cases and most recently in *Welch v. Bowmaker
(Ireland) Ltd.* ([1980] I.R. 251) that even if the subsequent chargee is
fixed with notice of the previous floating charge (as it must be registered according to section 99 of the 1963 Act) he can still retain priority if he can show that he had no awareness of the prohibition. It
would therefore be advisable for the lender to register a negative pledge
clause and protect his security in that way.

15.9   Crystallisation

In *Re Tullow Engineering (Holdings) Ltd.* ([1990] 1 I.R. 452), Blayney J.
stated that the floating charge is a form of security which takes imme-
diate effect, but allows the borrower to continue using the assets cap-
tured by it until crystallisation. Effectively, upon crystallisation the
floating charge becomes a fixed charge as it is now attaching to specific property and the company can no longer deal with those assets.
A floating charge crystallises, *i.e.* the charge stops floating and becomes attached to assets over which it was granted when a receiver is
appointed, when the company is wound up or where the company
has ceased to do business as was held in *Re Woodruffes (Musical Instruments) Ltd.* ([1986] 1 Ch. 366). In that case, the company created two
floating charges over the same class of assets. In the second debenture, which was issued to a director, it stated that the charge would
crystallise when the director gave notice to the company. She subse-
quently did this and the bank who held the first debenture appointed
a receiver. The court had to assess which charge crystallised first. They
found that when the director had given notice, that the second charge
would crystallise, the company ceased to do business and therefore
the bank's charge also crystallised at that time. As the bank's charge
was registered first in time, it had priority. Technically, in Ireland the
case of *Halpin v. Cremin* ([1954] I.R. 19) is still law, and it states that
crystallisation will only occur if there is a winding up or upon the
appointment of a receiver. In other jurisdictions, including England,
it has been accepted that automatic crystallisation clauses could be

included in debentures stating that the charge would crystallise on a given event. These clauses have been criticised in that crystallisation could occur without the company or other creditors being aware of it. However, in *Re Brightlife Ltd.* ([1987] 2 W.L.R. 197), the English courts upheld an automatic crystallisation clause which required notice to be given to the company by the chargeholder. They said that the creation of a charge was a contractual arrangement between the parties and that this could be upheld. It has been held by the Supreme Court in *Re Holidair Ltd.* ([1994] 1 I.L.R.M. 481) that a floating charge which has crystallised will decrystallise on the appointment of an examiner to the company, so that it ceases to be a fixed charge and reverts back to being a floating charge.

15.10   Retention of title clauses

A company may have assets on its balance books which have not been paid for and over which there is a purported retention of title clause, *i.e.* the supplier has stated that the rights and title to the property are retained until such time as the company pays for the goods. Therefore, a creditor with a charge over assets may find that some of the assets are not actually owned by the company. These *simple* retention of title clauses have been upheld by the courts in favour of the suppliers, provided that the assets or materials as supplied are still identifiable and in their original state, *e.g. Frigoscandia (Contracting) Ltd. v. Continental Irish Meat Ltd.* ([1982] I.L.R.M. 396). However, in many cases the courts have had to assess the validity of these clauses where the raw materials supplied have been converted into a finished product or where the materials have been sold on. In the case where the raw materials have been converted into a finished product, the *aggregate* retention of title clause has not been upheld and instead the courts have held that the buyer company creates a charge over the finished product in favour of the supplier. In many cases, as in *Kruppstahl AG v. Quitman Products Ltd.* ([1982] I.L.R.M. 551), the court held that a retention of title clause did not exist, but rather that the company had created a charge in favour of the supplier, which was void because it was not registered (see 15.11 below). Also, where the clause claims to reserve title over the proceeds of sale of the goods the courts have held that a charge is created in favour of the supplier and that that charge must be registered. The equitable remedy of tracing may be open to the supplier in relation to the proceeds, but this depends on whether a fiduciary relationship exists between the buyer and the seller.

In *Carroll Distributors Ltd v. G. & J.F. Bourke Ltd.* ([1990] I.L.R.M. 285), the courts held that the existence of a retention of title clause did not in itself prove the existence of such a relationship.

15.11 Registration of charges

It is essential that a company registers any charges which have been created over its assets so that parties dealing with the company can assess the status of the company's assets. Section 99 of the Companies Act 1963 requires that a charge be registered with the Registrar of Companies within 21 days of its creation. Section 100 requires the company to carry out this task, but it is advisable that the lender should register the charge himself as it is in his interest to do so. If a charge which should be registered is not registered, the law would declare the charge void as against the liquidator and other creditors and the chargeholder becomes an unsecured creditor who has no form of priority on winding up. Therefore, a later chargee can register his charge and gain priority over an earlier unregistered charge of which he is aware. If a charge is void for non-registration, the company must still repay the money and, under section 99(1), the money secured becomes immediately repayable.

Section 99(3) of the Companies Act 1963 sets out a number of charges which must be registered in order to acquire priority over others which include, *inter alia*, charges for the purpose of securing any issue of debentures; charges created by instruments akin to a bill of sale; charges on book debts of the company; floating charges; charges on calls made but not paid; judgment mortgages; charges created on property in Ireland by foreign companies; and charges .on ships or goodwill. Section 99(10) sets out that mortgages must also be registered as charges for the purposes of priority. Section 122 of the 1990 Act provides that the Minister can add new descriptions of charges which must.be registered.

The Registrar must record the date of creation of the charge which may be of huge significance if there are a number of floating charges, the amount secured by the charge, short particulars of the property charged and the persons entitled to the charge. Section 104 of the Companies Act 1963 requires the Registrar to give a certificate that the charge is registered in pursuance of the Act and the certificate is then conclusive evidence that the charge has been registered accordingly. This was so held in *Lombard & Ulster Banking Ltd. v. Amurec Ltd.* ((1978) 112 I.L.T.R. 1). In certain cases of fraud, or where there is error on the face of the certificate, the courts in England have left open the possibility of challenging the certificate.

15.12   Late registration of charges

Under section 106 of the Companies Act 1963, the court has jurisdiction to extend the time for registration of a charge under section 99 and to rectify any omission or error in the particulars provided. The courts have to be satisfied that the failure to register within the 21 days was:

> "accidental, or due to inadvertence or some other sufficient cause or is not of a nature to prejudice the position of other creditors or shareholders or the company or that on other grounds it is just and equitable to grant relief."

The order extending the time will extend time for registration until a certain date and will always contain a proviso that it is without prejudice to creditors who acquired rights prior to the registration, *i.e.* those who acquired charges within the period of time since the original charge was created and the date of its actual registration. This means that, whilst the lender is protected by getting his charge registered eventually, he cannot have priority over those who had registered charges in the period between the creation and registration of his charge. It has been held in England in *Re Resinoid & Mica Products Ltd.* ([1983] Ch. 132) and *Victoria Housing Estates Limited v. Ashpurton Estates Ltd.* ([1983] Ch. 110) that an order extending the time cannot be made once the company has been wound up, save in the most exceptional circumstances. If a winding up is imminent, the court may well grant the order extending the time for registration but will require an undertaking from the applicant that if the company is wound up within a month of the extension order being made and the liquidator applies within 21 days to have the order discharged, that the applicant would submit to the jurisdiction of the court. In *Re Telford Motors Ltd.* (unreported, High Court, January 27, 1978), the court set aside the late registration once the liquidator applied upon winding up. Hamilton P. said that the unsecured creditors had acquired rights once the winding up order was made and were entitled to the benefit of the proviso in section 106.

16. RECEIVERSHIP

If a company fails to make repayments on a loan, the debenture holder has a number of options open to him. If he is an unsecured creditor, with no proprietary interest in any of the company assets, he can bring proceedings for the recovery of the money and seek judgment in that regard, or he can petition the court to wind up the company. However, if the debenture is secured by a fixed or floating charge then it will be written into the debenture that the debenture holder can appoint a receiver at any time after the principal monies which were secured become payable. The receiver, when appointed, will go into the company and receive and take control of those assets which are the subject of the debenture holder's charge. The receiver can then dispose of those assets and pay off the principal and interest due to the debenture holder. The particular debenture will set out the instances on which the principal monies become payable, *e.g.* after six months default of payment, on an order for a winding up of the company; if a receiver is appointed over the whole undertaking of the company; or if the company ceases or threatens to cease to do business. Often a receivership can be followed by liquidation, and in many instances receivership can be welcomed by the company directors who fear that they are unable to pay their debts and do not wish to trade on and incur personal liability.

16.1 Appointment of a receiver

The receiver is usually appointed by virtue of the debenture and it is normally written into the debenture that the receiver, who is appointed by the particular debenture holder shall be an *agent* of the company and that the company is solely responsible for the acts or defaults of the receiver and for his remuneration. If there is no such provision, the receiver will be deemed to be the agent of the debenture holder. The court also possesses an inherent power to appoint a receiver on application by a debenture holder. An application may have to be made to court to appoint a receiver in instances where the debenture does not provide for an appointment in a particular situation which has arisen. A receiver who is appointed by the court is an *officer of the court* and is not an agent of the company or the debenture holder, yet he does owe the same fiduciary duty to the debenture holder in the exercise of his duty. At common law, the appointment of a receiver by the court had in the past resulted in all of the company's employees being dismissed, but now the European Communities (Safeguarding of Employees Rights on Transfer of Undertakings) Regulations 1980 protect the rights of employees, regardless of the fact that a receiver has been appointed. Certain persons cannot act as a receiver of the company including undischarged bankrupts and persons connected with, or related to, persons within the company (section 170 of the 1990 Act), and there is a fine for acting if not entitled to do so. A receiver who is appointed by debenture can resign with notice whereas a receiver appointed by the court can only resign with the authority of the court.

16.2   Consequences of appointment

When a receiver is appointed on foot of a debenture which is secured by a fixed charge, the receiver can just go in and realise that particular specific asset and dispose of it in order to pay off the debenture holder. If the debenture is secured by a floating charge, then the floating charge will crystallise and become a fixed charge on the assets or undertaking over which it was created. The company's and the directors' powers over these assets are suspended, and they cannot then deal with these assets without the receiver's consent. In *Lascombe Ltd. v. United Dominions Trust (Ireland) Ltd.* ([1994] 1 I.L.R.M. 227), the court stressed that the directors still retained their powers as directors in relation to assets not covered by the receiver's charge and in that case were entitled to initiate proceedings against a creditor.

16.3   Powers and duties of the receiver

The receiver will usually be given the power to manage the company, as it is in this way that he will be able to realise the value of the assets. This would be the case where the receiver is appointed over the whole undertaking of the company on foot of a floating charge. The receiver may be given powers in the court order or debenture to do all that is necessary to realise the security, *e.g.* to sue for the property charged, to carry on the business and raise money in that regard, execute conveyances in the company name and to make appropriate compromises. Section 178 of the 1990 Act enables a receiver to take action to recover assets which were wrongfully taken from the company. Under section 316 of the 1963 Act, as amended by section 171 of the 1990 Act, the receiver can apply to the court for directions on any aspect of his duty.

When the receiver is appointed, pre-existing contracts remain binding on the company, but the receiver is not personally liable in respect of these contracts unless there is a novation, *i.e.* the contract is renewed and the receiver takes on the obligations of the company. This has, in many instances, allowed the receiver to entirely disregard the company's contractual obligations. Section 316(2) of the Companies Act 1963 provides that the receiver is personally liable on any contract which is entered by him after he is appointed receiver, whether in his own name or in the name of the company.

The primary duty of the receiver is owed to the debenture holder who appointed him and a fiduciary relationship of trust is implied. He will therefore be liable to the debenture holder in damages if he is negligent in the conduct of the receivership. The receiver does, however, owe certain duties to the company for whom he acts as agent. Under section 316A of the 1963 Act, as inserted by section 172 of the 1990 Act, the receiver will be answerable to the company if he is negligent in the sale of company assets. The section provides that:

> "a receiver, in selling property of a company, shall exercise all reasonable care to obtain the best price reasonably obtainable for the property at the time of the sale."

The provision gave statutory effect to the law in Ireland at the time where it was felt that a receiver who was selling assets with one creditor in mind, should be required to ensure that he got the best price for an asset, even if a much smaller sum would realise his security. Other creditors would be looking to the excess to satisfy their debts. This was accepted in Ireland in *Lambert v. Donnelly* (unreported, November 1982) and *McGowan v. Gannon* ([1983] I.L.R.M. 16).

The English case of *Bank of Cyprus (London) Ltd. v. Gill* ([1980] 2 Lloyd's Rep. 51) dealt with a mortgagee's duty to get the best price at the time of sale, but is analogous to a receiver's duty. In that case, it was felt that the mortgagee did not have to wait for an upturn in the market, but was entitled to sell when getting the best price at the time.

Section 316A(3) of the 1963 Act, as inserted by section 172 of the Companies Act 1990, imposes a restriction on a receiver selling a non-cash asset of the company to anyone who was an officer of the company within three years of the receiver's appointment. He must give 14 days notice to all creditors of the company of this intention.

16.4   Publication of details of receivership

The receiver is not felt to have a duty to account to the company whose affairs he is managing. However, when a receiver is appointed and his appointment is published in *Iris Oifigiúil* and notified to the company, the company must provide him with a statement of affairs of the company within 14 days under section 319(1) of the 1963 Act. This will set out the company's assets and liabilities, etc. Failure to furnish a statement of affairs can result in fines. Within two months of the receipt of the statement, the receiver must send a copy of it to the Registrar, the company and the debenture holders with comments thereon. He must then continue to furnish the Registrar with abstract reports every six months setting out the status of the company, the assets which he has sold and the proceeds of such sales. Where the receiver is appointed, every letterhead of the company and every invoice must state that the company is in receivership.

16.5   Remuneration of the receiver

The remuneration of a receiver who is appointed by the debenture may be fixed by an agreement between the debenture holder and the receiver, whereas the receiver who is appointed by the court will have his remuneration fixed by the court.

16.6   Other matters concerning the receiver

Section 98 of the Companies Act 1963 provides that where a receiver is appointed under a floating charge, he must pay off preferential creditors, such as the Revenue and employee, out of the assets which he realises before he can pay the sum due to the debenture holder. In *United Bars v. Revenue Commissioners* ([1991] 1 I.R. 396), the assets being realised were subject to fixed and floating charges and Murphy J. held that where the receiver was left with a surplus after the sale, that the surplus was payable to the company and not to the preferential creditors. In *Re Eisc Teo* ([1991] I.L.R.M. 760), the court held that where a company had gone into liquidation after a receiver had received a surplus on the sale of assets, the receiver did not have to pay the surplus over to the liquidator, as he still had a statutory duty to apply the surplus in payment of the preferential creditors. Also, where a receiver is appointed under a floating charge, where the property is already the subject of a fixed charge, the floating charge must yield priority to the fixed charge and the receiver will not be able to sell the property without the consent of the fixed chargeholder.

Section 322B of the Companies Act 1963, as amended by section 176 of the 1990 Act, provides that if a creditor's winding up or a court-ordered winding up follows upon the appointment of a receiver, the liquidator can apply to court to have the receivership terminated and prohibit any other receiver from acting. This is due to the conflicting allegiances of the receiver, who is acting for one creditor and the liquidator who is seeking to realise assets for the benefit of all.

17. INVESTIGATION OF THE AFFAIRS OF THE COMPANY

17.1 Introduction

Prior to the enactment of the Companies Act 1990, the Minister for Enterprise and Employment was the only individual who could appoint an inspector to investigate the affairs of a company. The instances in which such a power could be used were extremely limited and successive Ministers were reluctant to use the power. Part II of the 1990 Act replaced sections 165–173 of the Companies Act 1963 and introduced various changes in the area:

(i) Section 7 of the 1990 Act confers a general power on the High Court to appoint an inspector to investigate the affairs of the company on the application of the company, a creditor or the members who hold not less than one-tenth of the paid up share capital. The court has discretion as to the circumstances in which an appointment should be made and shall set out the manner in which the inspector shall report to the court. The power to make an order under section 7 is limited to companies incorporated in Ireland. Section 7(3) enables the court to require the applicant to provide security for costs to avoid vexatious applications;

(ii) Section 8 of the 1990 Act confers a power on the High Court to appoint an inspector on the application of the Minister. The provision sets out that the appointment can only be made where the court is satisfied that there are, or have been, fraudulent practices within the company which have defrauded creditors or have been unfairly prejudicial to members or that the directors have been guilty of fraud, misfeasance or misconduct. The power to make an order under section 8 extends to companies incorporated outside Ireland;

(iii) Section 14 of the 1990 Act confers an extensive new power on the Minister to appoint an inspector to investigate *the ownership of a company, i.e.* to establish the true persons who are financially interested in the company. The power entitles the Minister to require the production of documents and to obtain search war-

119

rants for this purpose. This power is inherent in the
Minister and no court application is required.

Numerous investigations have been instigated in the past 10 years on
foot of the above powers, *e.g.* the National Irish Bank enquiry, the
Greencore enquiry and the Telecom Éireann enquiry. The latter enquiry was set up to enquire into the purchase of premises by Telecom
for £9.4 million in 1990, the same premises having changed hands
two years earlier for £4 million. The investigation sought to unravel
the chain of interlocking companies which had been involved in the
transaction.

17.2   Investigation

The investigations which are authorised under sections 7 and 8 of the
1990 Act permit an inspector to investigate the "affairs of a company" which includes the company's goodwill, its profits and losses,
its contracts and shareholdings and the control which it has over subsidiaries. The function of the inspector is to investigate and report
and, as a fact-finding exercise, the investigation is purely inquisitorial
in nature. The inspector will present his report to the court and the
court can make a series of orders on foot of the findings, *e.g.* disqualification of directors or winding up of the company. Despite the fact
that the inspector is acting on foot of a court order, he is not thought
to be exercising the judicial power of the State but rather to be carrying out an administrative function. However, the case of *Re Haughey*
([1971] I.R. 217) sets out that the inspectors must observe the constitutional requirements of fair procedures as the findings of their reports may have serious consequences for individuals within the company. In *Re Pergamon Press Ltd.* ([1971] Ch. 488), it was made clear that
the inspector must give an outline of the charge being put against a
company or individual to them in order that they can defend themselves prior to the report being given to the court. The inspector may
not need to conduct an oral hearing during the course of an investigation, but if he does the individuals called to give evidence are entitled
to legal representation and are also entitled to cross-examine witnesses
and have time to prepare their case (*Kiely v. Minister for Social Welfare*
([1977] I.R. 267)). In *Nolan v. Irish Land Commission* ([1981] I.R. 23), it
was deemed to be a breach of fair procedures to deny individuals the
access to documents which the inspector had acquired from other
parties in the course of the investigation.

17.3 Powers of inspectors

Inspectors appointed by the court have wide-ranging powers conferred on them to facilitate the investigation. Under section 9, they can apply to the court to extend their investigation of a named company to related companies (section 140, 1990 Act). Section 10(4) permits an inspector to compel the officers, agents or directors of the company to appear before him and be examined on oath. Section 10(1) places all officers of the named company under a duty to produce all relevant books and reports to the inspector and to give full assistance to the inspector. Section 10(3) permits an inspector to compel a director of the company to produce bank statements and accounts maintained by him, where the inspector has reasonable grounds for believing that there is some irregularity regarding payments into or out of the account. Section 10(5) provided that where an officer or agent refused to produce books or attend before the inspector, that the inspector could certify this refusal to the High Court who could look into the matter, hear evidence and then punish the offender in the same manner as if he had been in contempt of court. Section 10(6) provided that the court had the option also of *compelling* the individual to produce the books or appear before the inspector. *In Desmond v. Glackin (No.2)* ([1993] 3 I.R 67), the court held that section 10(5) was unconstitutional, but provided that section 10(6) was valid in so far as it permitted the court to order the individual to comply with the inspector's requirements. The costs of the investigation are deemed to be borne by the Minister for Justice, but the court can require that either the applicant or the company which is the subject of the report bear some of the costs.

17.4 The inspector's report

The inspector is required to make a report to the court on completion of the investigation, and in many cases the court orders that interim reports also be furnished. The court can then make such orders as it sees fit on the basis of the report. Obviously the court cannot impose sanctions which deprive an individual of trial in due course of law, but the court can forward the report to the Director of Public Prosecutions. As stated above, the court can also order the disqualification of persons or order the winding up of the company. The court can forward the report to the applicant, creditors or members of the company and other interested persons and can omit particular sections from the reports where it would unfairly damage a business reputation. Section 23(3) of the Act provides that the report is privileged and that no defamation actions can be brought on foot of it. Section 22 of the Act provides that a copy of the inspector's report is admissible in any legal proceedings as evidence of the opinion of the inspector and of the facts as set out therein. In *Countyglen Ltd. v. Carway,* (unreported, High Court, February 20, 1996), the defendants claimed that to permit the report be used as evidence of fact was unconstitutional because it would allow an inquisitorial report to override adversarial proceedings. Laffoy J. said that Section 22 was not unconstitutional as it merely allowed the report as proof of facts and did nothing more than impose the burden of proof on the defendants to prove otherwise.

17.5   The section 14 appointment

Section 14 permits the Minister to appoint an inspector to assess the true ownership of a company. The section sets out that the Minister must be satisfied that the circumstances justify an investigation, in that the effective administration of company law requires it, the public interest requires it or the Minister is compelled to appoint in order to effectively discharge his functions. The Minister could be judicially reviewed in relation to an appointment and be asked to specifically set out his reasons. In *Dunnes Store Ireland Co. v. Maloney* ([1999] 1 I.L.R.M. 119), Laffoy J. said that the Minister had to give reasons for compelling books and documents to be furnished under section 19, and that the same rule applied in relation to the actual appointment under section 14. The Minister-appointed inspector has the same powers as the court-appointed inspector in relation to the powers of discovery, publication, etc. However, unlike the court-appointed inspector under section 10(3), the Minister-appointed inspector cannot investigate the bank accounts of directors. The Minister is empowered under section 16 to prevent the transfer of shares after the inspector is appointed as this could frustrate the investigation. The Minister could require that information be furnished to him prior to the appointment of an inspector so that an assessment can be made as to whether he should appoint an inspector or apply to court for an appointment.

18. WINDING UP – LIQUIDATIONS

18.1 Introduction

A company's legal existence can be terminated by striking the company off the register or by liquidating the company. In Chapter 13, we looked at the power of the Registrar to strike companies which were either defunct or had failed to make annual returns for a number of years off the Register. In this chapter, we will examine the reasons why companies are wound up, the various forms which the liquidation can take and the consequences of liquidation. In a liquidation, the assets of the company are collected and realised, with the proceeds of sale being used to discharge the debts of creditors. The members will receive the balance, if any, which is outstanding after the costs and expenses of the liquidation have been paid off. Companies can be wound up for a number of reasons including: the company may be insolvent, the members may wish to liquidate the assets and receive the full return on their investment, there may be a breakdown in the effective running of the company, or the company may have completed the task which it was set up to complete and have no other function (section 251(3), 1963 Act).

There are three major ways in which a company can be wound up. If the company is solvent, the members can wind up the company themselves in a *members' voluntary winding up*. If the company is insolvent, the members may pass a resolution to wind up the company and the creditors will then take control of the winding up, *i.e.* a *creditors' voluntary winding up*, and finally, the High Court can order that the company be wound up upon receipt of a petition, *i.e.* a *compulsory winding up*. It must be noted that the forms of voluntary winding up are obviously much quicker and less expensive than the court procedure. The Companies Acts 1963–90 set out comprehensive rules regarding the different forms of winding up and also provide general rules which apply in relation to all forms.

18.2 Voluntary winding up

18.2.1 Members' voluntary winding up

Section 251(1) of the Companies Act 1963 provides that a company can be wound up "if the company resolves by special resolution that it should be wound up voluntarily". This may occur where the members simply wish to liquidate their investment or where they feel that the business does not have a long-term future, but the company must be solvent at the time of the resolution being passed. This requirement obviously seeks to protect creditors who could be prejudiced by the winding up. Within the 28 days prior to this special resolution being passed, the majority of the directors are required, under section 256 of the 1963 Act, to make a statutory declaration of the solvency of the company, *i.e.* that the company will be able to pay its debts within at least 12 months from the commencement of the winding up. The declaration must also contain a statement of the assets and liabilities of the company as at the date prior to the declaration. Directors can be held personally liable for the debts of the company for making a declaration of solvency when there were no reasonable grounds for so doing. Section 128 of the 1990 Act amends the section by adding the requirement that an "independent person" must make out a report also verifying that the company is solvent. The special resolution passed by the company must then be published. The date of the commencement of the winding up is the date on which the resolution was passed.

The members must then appoint a liquidator at a general meeting, who must consent to such appointment, and the members must fix his remuneration. Section 258(2) of the 1963 Act provides that all of the powers of the directors cease on the appointment of the liquidator except in so far as the company or the liquidator sanctions their continuance. The liquidator's job is to realise all the assets of the company, pay off creditors and then distribute the remaining proceeds amongst the members. The liquidator is under an obligation to call meetings of the members throughout the liquidation, and is obliged under section 263 to call a final general meeting when the liquidation is complete to inform the members of the situation. The company is deemed to be dissolved three months after the final accounts are submitted to the Registrar.

18.2.2   *Creditors' voluntary winding up*

A creditors' voluntary winding up involves the creditors appointing a liquidator and fixing his remuneration. The creditors' voluntary winding up can arise in a number of ways. First, if the company is insolvent, under section 251(2) of the 1963 Act, the members may pass an ordinary resolution that the company be wound up and may appoint a liquidator at that meeting. However, section 266 of the 1963 Act requires the company to call a meeting of the creditors on the same day as the members meeting, or the day after, to inform them of the situation and place a statement of all of the accounts and liabilities before the creditors. The company are also required to publish notice of this meeting in newspapers. Whilst the creditors may agree that the liquidator appointed by the members shall act as liquidator, it is more common that they appoint a liquidator themselves, and from that point on, the winding up becomes a *creditors' winding up*. The appointed liquidator must consent to so acting. Section 131 of the 1990 Act places great restrictions on the liquidator who is appointed by the members in the short period prior to the creditors' meeting, as it would otherwise be possible for the nominee of the members to act in a manner prejudicial to the creditors in the period of time prior to the creditors being made aware of the situation. The creditors can then appoint a committee of inspection which shall fix the remuneration of the liquidator and also monitor the winding up. This committee is made up of nominees of the creditors and it enables the creditors to supervise the liquidation. The liquidator must call meetings of the members and creditors throughout the winding up, and again present a final account to the meetings. As with the members' winding up, the company is deemed to be dissolved within three months of the final account being submitted to the Registrar.

A winding up may commence as a members' winding up with the necessary declaration of solvency, but under section 256(3) of the 1963 Act, a creditor or creditors representing one-fifth of the creditors in number or value can apply to the court to have the winding up continued as a creditors' winding up. The court will grant the order if they are satisfied that it is unlikely that the company will be able to pay its debts within the period specified in the declaration of solvency. A *members' voluntary winding up* can also be converted into a *creditors' winding up* under section 129 of the 1990 Act. This section provides that the members' liquidator must call a creditors' meeting where, in the course of winding up, he forms the opinion that the company is *not* able to pay its debts and that the creditors must therefore be given the opportunity to take over. In these two instances, the rights of the creditors are being safeguarded because the company is actually insolvent and their interests will be best served if they control the liquidation procedure.

18.2.3 *Powers and duties of liquidators in voluntary winding up*

The liquidator who is appointed in either of the above voluntary liquidations can exercise the same powers which are given to official liquidators appointed by the court. There are a few instances however, where the members' voluntary liquidator must get the sanction of the general meeting to act and where the creditors' voluntary liquidator must get the consent of the committee of inspection. These instances are set out in section 276(1) of the 1963 Act, *i.e.* where the liquidator proposes to pay off a class of creditors in full; where he proposes to compromise claims or make arrangements with creditors. All other powers which are generally given to the court liquidator are given to the voluntary liquidator, *inter alia*, bringing or defending actions in the company name; selling company property; borrowing money on the security of company assets and carrying on the business of the company. Under section 280 of the Companies Act 1963, the voluntary liquidator is permitted to apply to the court for guidance on any particular issue which arises in the course of the winding up. The liquidator is entitled to be furnished with all books and records in relation to the company when he is appointed. Under section 277 of the 1963 Act the court has the power to dismiss a liquidator where cause is shown, *e.g.* a conflict of interest or misconduct. There may be an increased possibility of such conflicts arising in the case of members' or creditors' voluntary winding up where the parties have appointed the individual in question and he may have failed to disclose connections to certain members or creditors. Under section 281 of the 1963 Act, the liquidator is entitled to have his costs and expenses of the liquidation paid in priority to all other claims.

18.3 Winding up by the court (compulsory winding up)

The High Court is empowered to make an order to wind up a company on the application of the company itself or any creditor, member or contributory of the company. The Minister can also present a petition to have a company wound up, as can any person who claims they are being oppressed under section 205 of the 1963 Act. The majority of such petitions are presented by creditors of companies who wish to have the court order a liquidation in instances where the company has not passed a resolution to wind up the company. If the court accedes to the application and appoints a liquidator, the liquidator will be deemed to be an officer of the court and whilst given extensive powers, will work under the supervision of the court. The court will fix the remuneration of the liquidator. It has been noted in the case of *Re Downs & Co.* ([1943] I.R. 420) that the fact that a company is already in voluntary liquidation does not prevent the court from making an order to wind the company up, upon application by a creditor. The court said that an order would be made where the petitioner showed that he would be prejudiced if the voluntary winding up continued. In a court-ordered winding up, as in a voluntary winding up, the liquidator will collect and realise the assets of the company and distribute them amongst the creditors. Application may be made to the court to determine questions of priority in relation to certain charges and securities. The court will also be called upon by the liquidator to examine the conduct of the company directors prior to the winding up, and it is the liquidator who will bring the actions for reckless trading and misfeasance against the directors, as well as applications for restriction and disqualification of directors. It is noted that there is greater likelihood of such actions being brought by a court-appointed liquidator than by a voluntary liquidator.

18.3.1   *Grounds for court-ordered winding up*

The court has the authority to wind up all forms of companies registered under the Companies Acts and former Acts, as well as unregistered companies such as friendly societies and savings banks. The grounds upon which the court can wind up a company are set out in section 213 of the 1963 Act, namely: where a company resolves by special resolution to have the company wound up in this way; where the company has not done business for a full year since incorporation or has suspended business for a year; where the number of members of the company has fallen below the statutory minimum; where the company is unable to pay its debts; where it is deemed to be "just and equitable" to wind up the company and where a member is being oppressed or his interests are being disregarded. The former grounds are seldom used, as in the first instance the company will more likely decide to wind up voluntarily and save money.

The most frequent ground for winding up is where the company is unable to pay its debts, section 213(e), and the petition claiming this is presented by a creditor. Section 214 of the 1963 Act, as amended by section 123 of the 1990 Act, provides that a company will be deemed to be unable to pay its debts in certain instances, *e.g.* where the creditor can prove that a debt in excess of £1,000 is owed to him and three weeks have elapsed since demand was made; where the creditor can prove that a judgment is unsatisfied and where the court is simply satisfied that on the evidence, the company is unable to pay its debts, *e.g.* the fact that a creditor has repeatedly sought repayment without return. The courts have set out, however, that this provision shall not be abused and that the application to have a company wound up cannot be a debt recovery process. If the company has substantial grounds to dispute the existence of the debt, the petition can be dismissed by the court, or if the company brings the matter to the court's attention prior to the issue of the petition, the issue can be restrained (*Re Pageboy Couriers Ltd* ([1993] I.L.R.M. 510)). In the case of *Truck & Machinery Sales Ltd. v. Marubeni Komatsu Ltd.* ([1996] 1 I.R. 12), the court said that the issue of a petition could be restrained where there would appear to be an ulterior motive for presenting the petition, but pointed out that the court would only restrain the issue in exceptional circumstances, because to do so was to deprive the creditor of access to the court. Under section 213(f), the court has a general discretion to wind up a company where it feels that it is *just and equitable* to do so. This discretion can be exercised on foot of a specific petition or the court can make such an order on foot of other proceedings. The court has granted such winding up orders where they have noted that the trust and confidence associated with a small private company has broken down (*Re Murph's Restaurant Ltd.* ([1979] ILRM 141)). In that case, two of the three director/shareholders were attempting to dismiss the third party and the court felt that the basis of trust and confidence within the company was gone and ordered a winding up so that the third shareholder could have access to his investment. The court has also granted orders under this heading where there is deadlock within the company (*Re Vehicle Buildings and Insulations Ltd.* ([1986] I.L.R.M. 239), where the company is being used as a vehicle for fraud or where the company cannot carry out its function any longer).

On foot of an application under section 205 of the 1963 Act by a member for oppression or disregard of interests, the court has the inherent jurisdiction to wind up a company. Also, section 141 of the Companies Act 1990 provides that where two or more related companies are being wound up, the liquidator of one company can apply to have the two companies wound up together. The court would have to be satisfied that the companies are indeed "related companies" as defined in the Act.

18.3.2   *The petition to wind up a company*

Most petitions are presented by company creditors, and the court, in considering the application, has to have regard for the wishes of the other creditors of the company. If other creditors oppose the petition, they should give substantial reasons for the opposition (*Re P & J Macrue Ltd.* ([1961] 1 All E.R. 302)). In *Re Bula Ltd.* (unreported, High Court, May 13, 1988), the court refused a petition to wind up a company as they were satisfied that the application was simply being made to negative the judgment mortgage of another creditor, and in that sense was an abuse of process. The petition must be presented to the High Court and a copy served upon the company. It is also essential to publish notice of the petition in *Iris Oifigiúil* and two newspapers at least seven days prior to the hearing of the petition. Anyone wishing to be heard at the hearing must send notice to the petitioner's solicitor.

18.3.3   *The winding up order and appointment of the liquidator*

If the court makes an order winding up the company, section 220(2) of the 1963 Act provides that the date of winding up is the date the petition was presented and not the date of the order. The petitioner is generally given costs, as are the company. Once the winding up order is made, a statement of the company's affairs must be filed in court in order to provide the liquidator with the necessary preliminary information in relation to the company. Sometimes the court appoints a provisional liquidator prior to the winding up order being granted. This would happen in cases where the assets of the company are in danger (section 226 of the Companies Act 1963). The official liquidator who is appointed by the court must publish notice of his appointment in *Iris Oifigiúil* and in two newspapers. Whilst the liquidator need not have any specific qualification, he is generally an accountant and cannot have been an officer or servant of the company within the 12 months prior to winding up. The court has the necessary power to dismiss a liquidator for cause shown (section 228 of the Companies Act 1963). Section 229 of the Companies Act 1963 provides that when the liquidator is appointed he must take all property of the company into his possession, including all documents relating to company property. Section 125 of the 1990 Act provides that no person can withhold documents from the official liquidator. It is quite common for the liquidator to be assisted in the winding up by a committee, which is made up of members and contributories. Once appointed, the principal duties of the liquidator are: collecting the company assets and protecting them; drawing up lists of creditors and contributories; realising assets; seeking court direction on disputed matters; paying off creditors and distributing the surplus, if any, amongst the company members.

19. THE REALISATION AND DISTRIBUTION OF ASSETS

19.1   Consequences of winding up

When a winding up commences, various transactions concerning the company are frozen, as it is from this date that the assets are held in trust for the creditors. Section 218 of the Companies Act 1963 provides that when an order for winding up is made, any disposition of company property is void and ineffective, unless the court directs otherwise. This includes all dispositions of property of the company made between the date of the petition and the date of the order. Generally, the court would allow such dispositions which are made in good faith and in the normal course of business to remain effective. However, in *Re Pat Ruth Ltd.* ([1981] I.L.R.M. 51), Costello J. refused to validate payments made into the company's overdrawn bank account after the date of the petition, as he felt that this was an attempt to prefer the bank over other creditors.

Section 222 of the 1963 Act provides that when a liquidator is appointed by the court, all actions against the company are automatically stayed, whereas the voluntary liquidator has to apply to court requesting the stay. The commencement of the winding up terminates the powers of the directors unless they continue in office for some limited purpose. Shares cannot be transferred upon commencement of a court winding up, yet the voluntary liquidator may permit shares to be transferred (section 255 of the 1963 Act). Under section 291 of the 1963 Act, a creditor who has issued execution against the company cannot retain the proceeds of execution, unless it was completed prior to the commencement of the winding up. Section 284(2) of the 1963 Act provides that any judgment mortgage which is registered against the company's land within three months prior to the winding up does not obtain any priority over other contract debtors. Also, the commencement of winding up causes all floating charges on the company's property to crystallise and, whilst a receiver can be appointed, he will not be in a position to manage the company in any way. Section 176 of the 1990 Act permits the liquidator to apply to court to have the receivership terminated if conflict is arising.

19.2   "Asset-swelling measures"

The main purpose of liquidation is to realise all of the assets of the company, distribute the proceeds amongst the creditors in order of priority, and then pay out the remaining surplus to members according to their rights of repayment. In order to carry out this task, the liquidator is given an extensive range of powers which seek to protect existing assets, and which also enable him to set aside certain securities and call back certain payments which have been made in the past, which have preferred certain creditors over others. In this way, the liquidator can maximise the fund from which the creditors can be paid.

19.2.1 Examination

In order to ensure that no property or assets remain unaccounted for, sections 245 and 280 of the Companies Act 1963 enable the court to call before it any person who is suspected of holding company property or being indebted to the company and the court can then compel them to pay over the money or deliver the property to the liquidator (section 245A, as inserted by section 127 of the 1990 Act).

19.2.2 Fraudulent disposal

Section 139 of the 1990 Act is an important provision which permits the liquidator to recover company property which had been disposed of in any way that defrauded the company, its creditors or its members.

19.2.3 Fraudulent preference

Section 286 of the 1963 Act, as amended by section 135 of the 1990 Act, permits the liquidator to render void any fraudulent transfer or disposition made by the company in the six months prior to the liquidation commencing which was made:

> "in favour of any creditor ... with a view to giving such creditor, or any surety or guarantor for the debt due to such creditor, a preference over other creditors."

This provision aims to prevent companies paying off a particular creditor on the eve of liquidation and leaving little for the remaining creditors. In order to have the transaction rendered void, the payment or transfer must have been made when the company was insolvent. It is up to the liquidator to prove the fraudulent intent to prefer which is quite difficult in the majority of cases. If the company shows, that it was pressurised into making the preferential payment or transfer, this may be enough to negative a fraudulent intent. Section 135 of the

1990 Act provides that where the preferential payment was made in favour of a director or connected person within the two years prior to liquidation, it can be set aside and there is a presumption, until proven otherwise, that the payment was fraudulent.

19.2.4   Invalidating floating charges

Section 288 of the 1963 Act, as amended by section 136 of the 1990 Act, is another important provision that allows the liquidator to set aside floating charges which have been created in the 12 months prior to liquidation where no additional funds were loaned to the company at the time when the charge was created. This provision aims to prevent unsecured creditors of the company, who foresee a winding up, compelling the company to register a charge in their favour, despite the fact that they have not loaned the company any further capital. Charges which were registered in the two years prior to winding up can be set aside when registered in favour of a connected person (section 289 of the 1963 Act). The charges will not be set aside where it can be proven that the company was solvent when the charge was created or, in the case of outside creditors, where additional funds were loaned at the time.

19.2.5   Disclaiming onerous obligations

Section 290 of the 1963 Act permits the liquidator to disclaim, with the leave of the court, any company property which is unsaleable or is unduly burdensome because of excessive covenants, etc. This power is usually used to terminate leases where the court is satisfied that performance of the obligations of the lease would be too burdensome for the company. The party against whom this disclaimer is actionable, *e.g.* the landlord, can prove for damage as a result of the reneging of the contract in the winding up.

19.2.6   Contribution of related companies

Section 140 of the Companies Act 1990 provides that the liquidator of a subsidiary company can apply to court to have the holding company be made partly liable for the unpaid debts of the subsidiary. Before such an order is made, the court would have to be satisfied that the related company had some role to play in the winding up of the subsidiary company, *e.g.* the subsidiary took care of an area of the business which involved significant risk. If such an order is made, it would greatly contribute to the fund from which the creditors can be paid.

19.2.7   *Contributions from contributories*

In realising the assets of the company, it is noted that the liquidator must obtain payment from the contributories of the company of the amount, if any, uncalled on their shares in the company. The contributories are therefore the company members. Section 207 of the 1963 Act provides that in the event of the company being wound up, every past and present member must contribute to the assets of the company to enable it to pay off its debts. This provision is qualified by the principle of limited liability, which limits each member's payment to that amount which remains unpaid on his shares.

19.3   Distribution of assets

When the liquidator has realised all of the company assets, he must then set about paying off the creditors of the company and settling any claims they may have against the company. The liquidator's costs and expenses in carrying out the liquidation must also be paid out from this general fund, and then any surplus or balance which remains can be distributed amongst the company's members and shareholders. If the company's liabilities exceed its assets, section 284 of the 1963 Act provides that creditors with secured or preferential claims must be paid off first. Section 283(1) of the 1963 Act requires all debts in a liquidation to be proven. This means that every legal claim against the company can be put before the liquidator. The Rules of the Superior Courts provide that the liquidator must publish a notice requesting all creditors to present their claims within a certain time period. In a court winding up, the High Court examiner can request that certain claims provide further proof of the debts owed. Section 231(1)(e) of the 1963 Act provides that the liquidator can make any compromise or arrangement with creditors of the company, but in a court winding up, this must be approved by the court, and in voluntary winding up, it must be approved by the members or creditors, depending on the nature of the winding up.

19.4   Assets or funds which are unavailable for distribution

Before examining the priority of claims upon winding up, it must be noted that there may be assets or funds within a company which are not available for distribution upon winding up. This is because the property or fund in question is held on behalf of someone else and is not therefore available for distribution. If a company has purchased goods which are the subject of a *simple retention of title clause*, this will mean that the supplier has retained title in the goods until the goods are paid for. If the company goes into liquidation prior to payment, and the goods are still in an identifiable state, the supplier can simply remove the goods, as the supplier has full title to the goods. In Chapter 15, we examined the complex retention of title clauses which the courts have interpreted as charges, with the result that the supplier must be placed in rank as an unsecured creditor if he does not have the charge registered.

If the company *holds property on trust* for someone else, then that property must remain separate from the distribution fund and can be directly removed by the trustee. Section 62 of the Civil Liability Act 1961 provides that the proceeds of a company's insurance policy shall be used to pay a third party where the company has been responsible for injuring the third party and the company is insured for the particular liability. Prior to this Act, such an individual had no recourse against the company which had become insolvent. In order to avail of this form of priority, the individual must have commenced the claim prior to the company being dissolved.

19.5   Payments to creditors

(1) The first type of creditor to have his debt satisfied upon winding up is the *secured chargeholder*. This creditor will have a mortgage, fixed charge or lien over the property of the company and can realise that specific property when the company is wound up. Whilst it is most common for the secured chargeholder to simply rely on his security, it is also open to him to prove in the winding up for the deficiency in value of the asset, if it has realised a lesser sum that that which was owed to him by the company. Fixed charges and mortgages must be registered in order to assume their priority as from the date of creation. The secured chargeholder has therefore ultimate security when the company is wound up.

(2) The *costs and expenses of the liquidator* must be paid out of the liquidation fund before any other preferred debts. Section 281 of the 1963 Act provides that this is the case in a voluntary winding up and in *Re Red Breast Preserving Co.* ([1958] I.R. 234), the court held that the same should apply in compulsory winding up. Disputes have arisen as to whether certain taxes which become payable during a winding up should be considered to be the costs of the liquidator and therefore

receive priority in payment. In a compulsory winding up, the expenses must be approved by the Examiner or the Taxing Master of the High Court.

(3) *Preferential creditors* are the next class to be paid out of the liquidation fund. The Revenue Commissioners, company employees and the rating authority are the parties who are classified as preferential creditors whose debts must be paid off in priority to all unsecured creditors and even in priority to floating chargeholders. Section 285(14) of the Companies Act 1963, as amended by section 134 of the 1990 Act, requires all preferential creditors to make their claims for preferential treatment within six months of advertisement for same. It is noted in section 115 of the Finance Act 1996 that the Revenue must be paid in priority to those who hold fixed charges on book debts. The preferential payments to employees include unpaid salaries, holiday pay, outstanding pension contributions, etc. Rates which were due in the 12 months prior to the liquidation are also preferential debts.

(4) *Floating chargeholders* are the next class to be paid off on liquidation. As noted above, their claims can be superseded by the preferential creditors. All floating charges will crystallise upon winding up, and therefore the first in time prevails if the charges are all created over the same assets or undertaking of the company. The floating charge may have included a negative pledge clause, restricting the company from creating a further charge of equal or greater value. This clause will only have effect if the subsequent chargeholder was aware of its existence. A floating charge which has crystallised prior to liquidation, *e.g.* where a receiver was appointed, may obviously be satisfied by the receiver, provided that the liquidator does not apply to have the receivership terminated.

(5) *Unsecured creditors* are the last class of creditors to be paid upon liquidation. They are creditors who have no form of security for the debt owed to them by the company, but have proved the existence of their debt to the liquidator.

19.6   Payments to members and contributories

If there is a surplus remaining after all of the creditors have been repaid, that amount will fall to be distributed amongst the members. Members who have dividends owed to them and are due capital repayment are classified as deferred creditors. As contributories, they are entitled to have the amount paid on their shares returned to them, provided that existing funds allow for this. If there is a surplus on this, then the amount paid to each will be in proportion to the nominal amount of the share capital held by each of them.

20. ACTIONS AGAINST DIRECTORS

20.1 Introduction

In the course of the winding up of the company, certain actions of directors may be examined by the liquidator and may be brought to the attention of the court if the action involves some form of wrong-doing on the part of the director. The legislature has created a number of charges or actions which can be brought against the directors on foot of a winding up. These actions seek to expose directors who have *abused their position within the company* or have *traded fraudulently* or *recklessly* in the carrying on of the company business. A finding of liability in relation to such actions will, in the first instance, impose personal liability for the debts of the company on the individual director and in certain instances could also impose criminal liability. As stated, the majority of actions against directors will be pursued upon the winding up of the company, because the liquidator will have had the opportunity to examine the affairs of the company in depth. However, actions can also be brought by creditors of the company who are in a position to prove their case as against the director. Mention shall also be made in this chapter of the action which can be taken against officers of the company for *insider dealing*. This action can be taken at any time by an individual shareholder who has suffered loss as a result of the actions of the insider, who will, in many instances, be a director or related officer of the company.

20.2 Fraudulent trading

Section 297 of the Companies Act 1963 introduced the concept of making a director personally liable for the debts of the company where he had been shown to be guilty of fraudulent trading. The section also provided that such conduct constituted a crime. Section 137 of the 1990 Act created a new section 297, and section 138 of the 1990 Act created section 297A.

20.2.1 Criminal liability

The new section 297 now deals solely with the imposition of criminal liability on a director who is found guilty of fraudulent trading. The section provides that where, in the course of winding up, it appears that the business of the company has been carried on with an intent to defraud creditors or any other person, any person who was knowingly party to this is guilty of an offence and is liable on summary conviction to imprisonment for up to 12 months and a fine of up to £1,000, and on indictment to up to seven years' imprisonment and a fine of £50,000 or both. The application can also be made where no winding up has yet taken place, but the applicant is in a position to prove that the company cannot pay its debts.

20.2.2   Civil liability

The new section 297A provides that a director can be held personally liable for the debts of the company where he is found to be guilty of fraudulent trading. The onus of proving the fraud lies with the applicant and is a difficult onus, which explains the introduction of the civil offence of *reckless trading*, also in section 297A. The part of section 297A which refers to civil liability in relation to fraudulent trading is relatively unchanged from the 1963 provision. Therefore, pre-1990 authorities can be referred to in assessing when liability is imposed. The provision applies to "any person" who was knowingly a party to the fraudulent trading and is not therefore limited to directors of the company. In Re *Aluminium Fabricators Ltd.* (unreported, High Court, May 13, 1983), O'Hanlon J. found the directors guilty of fraudulent trading where the directors had kept two sets of books in order to conceal from the Revenue, their creditors and their auditors that they had siphoned off assets of the company for their own benefit. In Re *Kelly's Carpetdrome Ltd.* (unreported, High Court, July 1, 1983), Costello J. found the controller of the company guilty of fraudulent trading as he had destroyed records and transferred assets in an attempt to defraud the Revenue. In both cases, the directors were held personally liable for all of the company's debts. In Re *Hunting Lodge Ltd.* ([1985] I.L.R.M. 75), the directors were held guilty of fraudulent trading, as in a single transaction, they had sold the single asset of the company and arranged for part of the purchase money to be paid into a separate account for their benefit. It was stated in that case that persons other than directors would only be found liable where they were an active party in the fraud and that mere inaction would not suffice. In O'Keeffe *v. Ferris* ([1993] 3 I.R. 165), the Supreme Court rejected a constitutional challenge to the imposition of the civil sanction of personal liability, stating that such was necessary to protect individuals who have been wronged as a result of the actions of the directors.

20.3   Reckless trading

The action against a director for reckless trading was introduced by section 297A of the 1990 Act. The onus of proving recklessness on the part of the director is clearly much less difficult than proving fraud and was therefore a welcome provision. The section provides that "any officer" of the company can be held personally liable for the debts of the company where it appears that, whilst he was an officer, he was knowingly a party to the carrying on of the business in a reckless manner. The application can be made by the liquidator, examiner or receiver and can also be made where the applicant can show that the company is unable to pay its debts as they fall due. If it is a creditor who seeks to bring this action, he must show that he has suffered loss or damage as a result of the action in question. Generally, such actions will be brought by the liquidator of the company in the course of the winding up. Subsection (2) of section 297A gives some form of explanation of what constitutes recklessness and provides that the officer can be deemed to be knowingly a party to reckless trading where:

> "... having regard to his knowledge, skill and experience that may reasonably be expected of a person in his position, that he ought to have known that his actions or those of the company would have caused loss to the creditors ... or ... he was party to the contracting of a debt and did not honestly believe on reasonable grounds that the company would be able to pay the debts as they fell due".

The officer's conduct is to be judged objectively and this was held by Lynch J. in *Re Hefferon Kearns Ltd. (No. 2)* ([1993] 3 I.R. 191). Lynch J. said that a director or officer would be found guilty of reckless trading where they were carrying on business and knew very well that there was an obvious and serious risk of damage to others. In that case, the court felt that the directors were potentially liable for contracting a debt when they did not honestly believe that it would be repaid, but the court relieved the directors of any liability by referring to subsection (6) of section 297A which provides that the court has a discretion to relieve directors where it is felt that overall they acted "honestly and responsibly". In *Re Hefferon Kearns* the fact that the directors had kept proper books of account, had personally guaranteed loans and had traded out of near insolvency before were all factors which the court took into account. It is felt that the actions of directors in trading on in the optimistic belief that the difficulties will pass could be deemed reckless, where the prudent director would have called a creditors' meeting to wind up.

20.4   Misfeasance proceedings

Section 298 of the 1963 Act as substituted by section 142 of the 1990 Act provides that in the course of winding up, actions can be taken against directors, managers, promoters or past or present officers of the company where there is evidence to show that they have misappropriated or retained company property or where they have been guilty of misfeasance or some other breach of duty. Effectively, the section provides that the director or officer be required to pay back or restore the company property or contribute to the assets of the company by way of compensation for the breach of duty. Misfeasance proceedings have been taken against directors where they have made secret profits, or where they have used funds of the company for objects other than those set out in the memorandum. In all cases, it must be shown that actual loss was suffered by the company, as the action does not provide a remedy for individual, aggrieved shareholders or creditors. In *Re Mont Clare Hotels Ltd.* (unreported, High Court, December 2, 1986), Costello J. said that a misfeasance action could not be brought against a director for a mere error of judgement and that something more than simple negligence was required to ground an action.

20.5   Insider dealing

Directors within a company can be hauled up on foot of the provisions contained in Part V of the 1990 Act which create an offence of insider dealing and which can impose both criminal and civil liability. The offence seeks to prevent parties within a company using privileged information in relation to the company shares and thereby selling shares or dealing in shares and making a profit as a result of the transaction. As we know, directors are required to disclose all interests in shares and are prevented by the Companies Acts from dealing in share options, *i.e.* section 30 of the 1990 Act. Part V of the 1990 Act provides individual shareholders, who have suffered a loss as a result of the transaction, with an action against the insider who may often be a director. Section 108 of the 1990 Act prohibits share dealings by persons who have in the past six months been connected with the company and are in possession of information which was not generally available, but if it were, would materially affect the price of the shares or securities. Therefore, under section 109(1) of the 1990 Act, the individual who has sold his shares without the benefit of this information can sue the "insider" for the difference in price which he accepted for the shares and that which he could have got had he been in possession of the relevant information. Under this section the insider is also required to account to the company for any profit which he acquires through dealing in the securities. Section 111 of the 1990 Act provides that criminal liability can also be imposed upon the insider who has manipulated the transaction, and hefty prison sentences and fines can be imposed in this regard, *i.e.* a maximum of 12 months' imprisonment or £10,000 fine on summary conviction, or 10 years' imprisonment or £50,000 fine on indictment. These penalties reflect the seriousness of the crime. The Companies (Amendment) (No.1) Act 1999 creates certain exceptions to the offence, *e.g.* where the price of a new share issue is stabilised at a specified price or where a government minister or the Central Bank enter into transactions in attempts to establish monetary, exchange rate or national debt management policies.

21. EXAMINERSHIP

21.1 Introduction

The concept of examinership was introduced into Irish law by the Companies (Amendment) Act 1990. This legislation was enacted in order to provide companies which were in financial difficulties with the chance of recovering and thereby avoiding liquidation. The legislation provides that application can be made to the court by the company, its directors, members or creditors seeking the appointment of an examiner. The appointment of an examiner would then place the company under the protection of the court for a specified time, in which time schemes and proposals were to be devised to facilitate the survival and recovery of the company. As a result of this court protection, the company could not be wound up, creditors could not realise securities, orders could not be made against company property, and proceedings could not be brought against company guarantors for realisation of debts. If a successful scheme was devised and compromises made with existing creditors, it would be possible for the company to survive, but in many instances the ailing company could not be saved and liquidation followed upon the examinership. It is noted that the Act was introduced in 1990 in a hurried attempt to prevent the collapse of the Goodman group of companies which would have resulted in a crisis in the meat industry. Due to strong criticism of some of the key provisions, the Act has been amended in several respects by the Companies (Amendment) (No. 2) Act 1999 which will be discussed below.

21.2 The grounds for appointing an examiner

An examiner can be appointed where the petitioner has shown that the company is, or is likely to be, unable to pay its debts and where there is no winding up in being at the time. By virtue of section 12 of the Companies (Amendment) (No. 2) Act 1999, it is now a legislative requirement that the court must be satisfied that there is a *reasonable prospect* of the survival of the company before they appoint an examiner. This section addresses one of the criticisms of the 1990 Act which provided that the court could appoint an examiner where this was *likely to facilitate* the survival of the company as a going concern. It was felt that this threshold was much too low and would allow for the appointment of an examiner where there was no realistic possibility of saving the company. Because the appointment of an examiner has such a major effect on the rights of creditors during that period, and because of the increased liabilities which the examiner could create in his time in office, it was repeatedly pointed out that examiners should not be appointed unless there were clear indications that there was a real prospect of saving the company. The legislature has adopted the approach which was applied by Lardner J. in *Re Atlantic Magnetics Ltd. (in receivership)* ([1993] 2 I.R. 561) where he advocated that a strict test requiring a reasonable prospect of survival be used. In that case, the Supreme Court had overruled Lardner J. believing that the examiner could be appointed where there was *some prospect of survival.*

21.3   The petition seeking appointment of an examiner

The petition can be presented to court by the company, its directors, creditors or members holding over one-quarter of the voting rights. In practice, most applications will be made by the company or the directors, as it is unlikely that a creditor would wish to have his right to realise his securities suspended by the appointment of an examiner. It is more likely that he would seek to appoint a receiver if he is a se-cured creditor or seek to have the company wound up. The 1990 Act required that the petition be supported by evidence that the company could possibly be saved by the court intervening and creating a pro-tection period, but there was no requirement for a detailed analysis of the company's situation to be presented to the court prior to the ap-pointment. This was another area of criticism of the 1990 Act, *i.e.* that an examiner was appointed when the court had no accurate re-port of the state of the company. Instead, the examiner himself was required to furnish the court with an interim report three weeks after his appointment. Section 7 of the Companies (Amendment) (No. 2) Act 1999 inserts a new section 3(3A) into the 1990 Act and now re-quires that rather than have a report presented by the examiner three weeks after the appointment, the petition should actually be accom-panied by the report of an *independent accountant* at the outset, setting out a statement of affairs of the company, its assets and liabilities, its creditors and securities and any discrepancies in management of the company property. The principal object of the report is to inform the court whether, in the opinion of the independent accountant, there is a *reasonable prospect of survival.* The report must set out the possible schemes of arrangement which may be met and must also set out the amount of funding which will be required to enable the company to trade on. The report should also set out any specific pre-petition debts which should be paid. This addresses the problem that, even when an examiner is appointed, the directors retain their powers and could end up being pressurised into paying off some creditors. The 1999 Act provides that only those debts referred to in the report should be paid. Section 9 of the 1999 Act provides that in exceptional circumstances, where the survival of the company is threatened, and where an independent report has not been prepared, the court can go ahead and appoint an examiner for a maximum period of 10 days. This discretion will not be used lightly and it is likely that exceptional circumstances will be limited. After the report is presented, the court can then continue the examinership by the set period of 70 days.

The petition must nominate an examiner who must have given his consent to act. If a creditor is making the application, he must provide security for the costs of the application (section 3(5) of the 1990 Act). Notice of the petition must be given to the Registrar of Companies and now, under section 10 of the 1999 Act, the court cannot appoint an examiner nor dismiss a petition without having given any creditor who has expressed a wish to be heard, an opportunity to be heard. However, section 3(7) of the 1990 Act still provides that the court can make an interim order and this will not be affected by the requirements of section 10. Section 4 of the 1990 Act provides that the court can make an order appointing an examiner over a related company providing that all conditions deeming the company to be related are met. If an examiner is appointed, the period of appointment will be 70 days, which can be extended by a period of 30 days and no more. The 1990 Act had provided for a protection period of 90 days, but the fact that the independent report is now presented at the petition stage, rather than the examiner presenting a report three weeks after appointment, explains the decreased period. Section 14 of the 1999 Act provides that the extra period of 10 days is allowed where the report of the independent accountant was not ready in time for presentation with the petition.

21.4   The appointment of the examiner

If the court is satisfied on foot of the petition and report that there is a reasonable prospect of survival of the company, the nominated examiner will be appointed. When he is appointed, the company is placed under the protection of the court and is removed from the remit of its creditors. The company cannot be wound up. No receiver can be

appointed, and if a receiver was appointed within the three days prior
to the appointment he can be removed. No judgments can be ordered
against company property, no securities can be realised and no proceedings can be taken against anyone who acted as guarantor for the
company. The directors still retain their management powers within
the company. These last two consequences of the appointment have
been criticised, but still remain in place in the 1999 Act. It is noted
that the value of debentures is greatly affected by the examinership
provisions, which override the appointment of the receiver who is
appointed within the three days prior to examinership. Section 17 of
the 1999 Act provides that whilst a floating charge receiver would
have been required to pay off the Revenue before giving the realised
sums to the debenture holder under section 98 of the 1963 Act, the
examiner will not be under that obligation. In *Re Holidair Ltd.* ([1994]
1 I.L.R.M. 481), it was established that if an examiner was appointed
within three days of the receiver being appointed on foot of the floating charge, the floating charge would de-crystallise and return to its
status as a floating charge.

21.5   The examiner – qualification, remuneration and expenses

The examiner who is appointed need not have any particular qualification, but will generally be a qualified accountant. He, like a liquidator, cannot have been an officer of the company within the previous
12 months. The court fixes the remuneration of the examiner, and he
is also entitled to the costs of carrying out the examinership. He can
employ staff to assist him, but has recourse to the company staff for
such purposes.

Section 10 of the 1990 Act provided that:

> "any liabilities incurred by the company during the protec-
> tion period which are referred to in subsection (2) shall be
> treated as expenses properly incurred by the examiner".

The liabilities referred to in subsection (2) were those liabilities certified by the examiner at the time they were incurred as liabilities which
were required in order to facilitate the survival of the company as a
going concern. These liabilities would include new borrowings by the
examiner etc. Section 29 of the 1990 Act had then provided that these
certified liabilities and expenses had to be paid in priority to all creditors, secured or unsecured, where a scheme of arrangement was drawn
up or a winding up ensued. This provision was one of the most criti-

cised in the 1990 Act, as it was deemed to subvert the whole lending process, in that secured creditors lost priority to the new liabilities and expenses incurred by the examiner in the examinership. This meant that if the examinership failed, as could well be the case, the secured lenders were greatly prejudiced. Therefore, section 28 of the 1999 Act now provides that these newly-incurred expenses only enjoy priority over ordinary creditors and not secured creditors. The court had emphasised in *Re Don Bluth Entertainment* ([1994] 3 I.R. 141) the need for care and expertise by the examiner in certifying liabilities, *i.e.* he should only certify those liabilities which are necessary to facilitate the survival of the company and only those which occur during the period of protection. This would apply today and it would also be advisable for the examiner to put all certification in writing.

It is noted that the remuneration and costs of the examiner, which are distinct from the certified expenses, are to be paid in priority to all creditors secured and unsecured, and this has been held to be so in *Re Springline Ltd.* ([1997] 1 I.R. 46). In that case, it was also established that the examiner's costs had to be paid in priority to those of a liquidator who was appointed when the examinership failed.

21.6   The powers and duties of the examiner

In the 1990 Act, the examiner had the duty to report on the state of the company and then at a later date present proposals and schemes of arrangement which had been made with the members and creditors. Since the 1999 Act provides that the report be made pre-examinership, the duties of the examiner now are simply to formulate proposals for a compromise and carry out such duties as the court may direct him to carry out. The examiner must report to the court within 35 days of his appointment informing it as to whether he has been able to come up with any schemes, etc. At this instance, if the court is not satisfied, it could order that the company be wound up (section 22 of the 1999 Act). The examiner has a number of powers during the examinership: he can require production of documents from any persons; require assistance from any officer of the company; call board meetings and attend same; and he can also apply to court under section 7(6) of the 1990 Act seeking clarification on any issue which arises during the examinership. Under section 9(1) of the 1990 Act, the court could make an order transferring all of the directors' powers of management to the examiner exclusively. The court will only make such an order where it is just and equitable to do so, as the directors normally retain their powers of management throughout the examinership. If the examiner is given these powers of management, he could then sell company assets. Section 11 of the 1990 Act provides that the examiner could sell assets which are the subject of floating charges, but that the chargeholder will have the same priority in relation to the proceeds of sale. The 1999 Act provides that an examiner cannot repudiate a contract which has been entered into prior to his appointment. The examiner has personal liability on any contracts entered into by him after his appointment.

21.7 Schemes of arrangement

In order to facilitate compromises and schemes of arrangements with creditors, it is necessary for the examiner to call meetings with the creditors and with members. A creditors' committee may be appointed by the examiner to assist him in carrying out his functions. The members and creditors are placed into different classes for the purposes of voting on the schemes of arrangement and these schemes are deemed to be accepted if the majority of each class vote in favour. When the proposals are put to the court, the court will have a hearing at which any creditor or member whose interests are impaired can be heard. The court will not approve the proposals unless at least one group of creditors whose interests are impaired vote in favour of the proposals, they are fair and equitable and not unfairly prejudicial. Obviously, creditors may be accepting a great reduction on the liability due to them so they must be heard and the court will balance up competing interests. The court may propose modifications to the scheme and if they are significant, the members and creditors must then vote on the proposal again. If the scheme is unworkable and the court cannot approve it, the company will then be wound up. It is open to the examiner to initiate actions against directors for fraudulent and reckless trading following upon his examination of the company.

It is noted that the 1999 Act has made some necessary amendments to the procedure and it is hoped that, in future, examiners will only be appointed in the most promising of cases and that this will therefore protect the interests of creditors and others whose interests are suspended and often prejudiced by the fruitless examinership which eventually results in liquidation.

Index